PRINCE2™ MSP™

Team Management Skills for Project and Programme Managers

GW00585919

London: TSO

information & publishing solutions

Published by TSO (The Stationery Office) and available from:

Online
www.tsoshop.co.uk

Mail, Telephone, Fax & E-mail
TSO
PO Box 29, Norwich, NR3 1GN
Telephone orders/General enquiries: 0870 600 5522
Fax orders: 0870 600 5533
E-mail: customer.services@tso.co.uk
Textphone 0870 240 3701

TSO Shops
16 Arthur Street, Belfast BT1 4GD
028 9023 8451 Fax 028 9023 5401
71 Lothian Road, Edinburgh EH3 9AZ
0870 606 5566 Fax 0870 606 5588

TSO@Blackwell and other Accredited Agents

© The Stationery Office 2008

All rights reserved. No part of this publication may be reproduced, stored in a retrieval system, or transmitted in any form or by any means, electronic, mechanical, photocopying, recording or otherwise without the permission of the publisher.

Applications for reproduction should be made in writing to The Stationery Office Limited, St Crispins, Duke Street, Norwich NR3 1PD.

The information contained in this publication is believed to be correct at the time of manufacture. Whilst care has been taken to ensure that the information is accurate, the publisher can accept no responsibility for any errors or omissions or for changes to the details given.

Melanie Franklin and Susan Tuttle have asserted their moral rights under the Copyright, Designs and Patents Act 1988, to be identified as the authors of this work.

The Swirl logo™ is a Trade Mark of the Office of Government Commerce

PRINCE2™ is a Trade Mark of the Office of Government Commerce

The PRINCE2 Cityscape logo™ is a Trade Mark of the Office of Government Commerce in the United Kingdom and other countries

PRINCE® is a Registered Trade Mark of the Office of Government Commerce in the United Kingdom and other countries

MSP™ is a Trade Mark of the Office of Government Commerce

A CIP catalogue record for this book is available from the British Library

A Library of Congress CIP catalogue record has been applied for

First published 2008

ISBN 9780113310814

Printed in the United Kingdom by The Stationery Office, London

N5810794 c20 06/08

Contents

List of figures and tables

Acknowledgements

The ideas and content for this book are a result of our many years of experience in project and programme management. They are also a result of all the successes and failures we have had on our projects and programmes, and all of the stories and anecdotes we have collected over the years. However, we would specifically like to thank all of our colleagues, clients and associates whom we interviewed for this book (too numerous to mention), and Maurice Leppard and Lindsay Campbell for their many hours spent reading through the content.

REVIEWERS

Angela Berry	Information Services
Amanda Comber	Rabobank International
Elizabeth Dartmouth	Hampshire County Council
Kate Williams	Audit Commission

MATURITY MARK

The TSO maturity mark on the back cover will help you decide if this publication is positioned at the appropriate level for your requirements and provide a route map to progress with embedding the OGC best-practice guidance. This publication, *Team Management Skills for Project and Programme Managers*, is levels 2 and 3.

Level 2 is Repeatable (process discipline) – OGC guidance is used repeatedly.

Level 3 is Defined (institutionalized) – OGC guidance is defined/confirmed as a standard business process.

For more information on the TSO maturity mark and how it can help you, please visit www.best-management-practice.com

Introduction

1

1   Introduction

Anyone working on a project or programme will know the excitement of working together as a team to achieve a common goal, but will also have been frustrated by the myriads of problems that result from working with colleagues drawn from across the 'host' organization and any supplier organizations. Too often, project staff are not given training in team management because they do not have formal line-management responsibilities and do not have teams reporting to them on the corporate organization chart.

However, it could be argued that the team management responsibilities of project and programme managers are so much greater than a standard line-management role. This is because project and programme managers will need to form new teams for each stage or tranche of work and define objectives for each of these teams in line with the overall objectives of the project or vision of the programme. Also, projects – more than any other part of the organization – use the 'matrix management' approach, drawing resources from a variety of different reporting lines. Project managers can often find themselves leading teams of staff with far more experience, technical knowledge or years in the organization than they have.

An essential part of being a project or programme manager is the ability to be an effective team leader. The team leader adds value by bringing people together into partnerships and sub-teams that exploit their specialist knowledge and interpersonal skills. The team leader acts as a link between the team members and as a central point for receiving and distributing information to support existing relationships and to establish new ones.

This publication explores how the management of these teams is reliant on the power of the relationships that are established between the leader of the team and the team members, and the relationships that operate between the team members themselves. The factors that affect these relationships are explored, including the values, behaviours and motivations of the team leader and the team members.

1.1   THE AUDIENCE FOR THIS PUBLICATION

This publication provides an insight to leading teams within a project or programme environment. It focuses on managing team development and facilitating team interactions. Examples have been included to illustrate how effective team management can help lead to success. It will be of most use for managers who wish to understand how leading teams on a project or programme differs from that in a business-as-usual environment.

This publication forms part of a series of three publications, each highlighting a specific area of interpersonal skills demonstrated by effective project and programme managers:

- Communication skills
- Leadership skills
- Team management skills.

The intended audience for these publications is not restricted solely to those already working in project or programme management, but includes anyone who is impacted by projects within their day-to-day work. However, a basic understanding of what a project is, and the organization structure that underpins projects and programmes, has been assumed.

1.2   THE STRUCTURE OF THIS PUBLICATION

Leading a team involves relationship building between the team leader and each individual team member and development of relationships between all of the team members. These relationships form the 'team culture'. Chapter 2 defines team management and examines some of the factors that lead to the development of these team relationships. Chapter 3 examines how the tasks of the team are defined, agreed and pursued for each stage of a project or each tranche of a programme. This is a practical guide, and whilst it is not possible to definitively state how a team will behave at any point in the project lifecycle, it is possible to identify the key activities that a team leader must address. These activities are illustrated using an example project; the text is also supplemented with quotes from the managers interviewed for this publication. For each part of the lifecycle, three activities are explored:

- Team mission and direction
- Team roles, responsibilities and processes
- Team relationships.

Appendix A identifies different motivating factors for team members. Appendix B provides practical tips for successful team management and Appendix C explains the stages of team development.

1.3 WORKING WITHIN A PROJECT OR PROGRAMME MANAGEMENT ENVIRONMENT

A project is a temporary organization structure that is created to deliver outputs (products and services) that are justified on the basis that the benefits of having these outputs outweigh the cost of delivering them. A project team consists of several layers of management – from the key decision-makers to the project manager and the team manager(s). Each of these may form or lead sub-teams within the project. For example, the sponsor leads the sub-team of the decision-makers; the project manager leads the sub-team of team managers, who may then also lead a sub-team of producers. Because of the nature of projects, these teams are temporary and usually diverse, with members representing various departments within an organization and potentially third-party suppliers. Some

team members may be virtual, in that they are not located near enough to be present at any face-to-face meetings and are managed via email, conference calls or other technological tools. Additionally, the composition of the project team may change, depending on the specialist work and skills required at different points in the project. So the team may experience regular disruptions due to the changing nature of the team make-up itself.

A programme is a temporary organization structure that is created to coordinate and direct the implementation of a set of related projects and activities in order to deliver outcomes and benefits that will drive forward the achievement of an organization's strategy. Programme teams include the programme sponsor (also known as the senior responsible owner), the programme manager and the business change managers. This group of senior management is responsible for coordinating and leading the efforts of all the projects within a programme. They also lead the change within the operational environments to ensure that the changes are being entrenched in the organization and the resulting benefits are being realized.

The project and programme management terminology used in this publication is based on the suite of guidance developed by the Office of Government Commerce (OGC), aimed at helping organizations manage projects and programmes. Principally, the terminology has been drawn from two approaches:

- PRINCE2™
- Managing Successful Programmes (MSP™).

Terminology from these approaches is included in the glossary at the end of this publication.

Figures 1.1–1.3 provide an overview of the links between the two approaches and the lifecycle model that is used in Chapter 3.

Figure 1.1 Getting started – overview of the links between PRINCE2, MSP and the lifecycle model

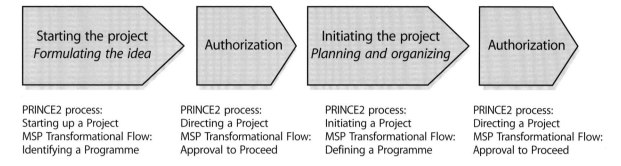

PRINCE2 process:
Starting up a Project
MSP Transformational Flow:
Identifying a Programme

PRINCE2 process:
Directing a Project
MSP Transformational Flow:
Approval to Proceed

PRINCE2 process:
Initiating a Project
MSP Transformational Flow:
Defining a Programme

PRINCE2 process:
Directing a Project
MSP Transformational Flow:
Approval to Proceed

Figure 1.2 Making progress – overview of the links between PRINCE2, MSP and the lifecycle model

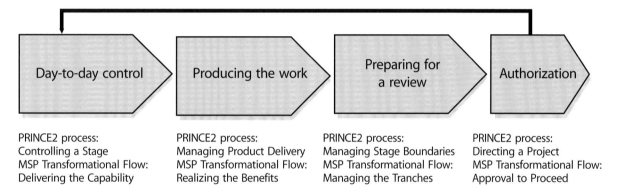

PRINCE2 process:
Controlling a Stage
MSP Transformational Flow:
Delivering the Capability

PRINCE2 process:
Managing Product Delivery
MSP Transformational Flow:
Realizing the Benefits

PRINCE2 process:
Managing Stage Boundaries
MSP Transformational Flow:
Managing the Tranches

PRINCE2 process:
Directing a Project
MSP Transformational Flow:
Approval to Proceed

Figure 1.3 Closing down – overview of the links between PRINCE2, MSP and the lifecycle model

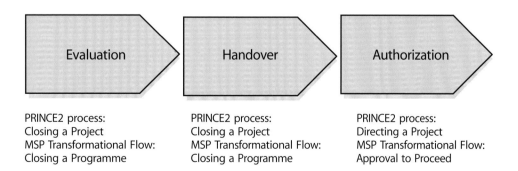

PRINCE2 process:
Closing a Project
MSP Transformational Flow:
Closing a Programme

PRINCE2 process:
Closing a Project
MSP Transformational Flow:
Closing a Programme

PRINCE2 process:
Directing a Project
MSP Transformational Flow:
Approval to Proceed

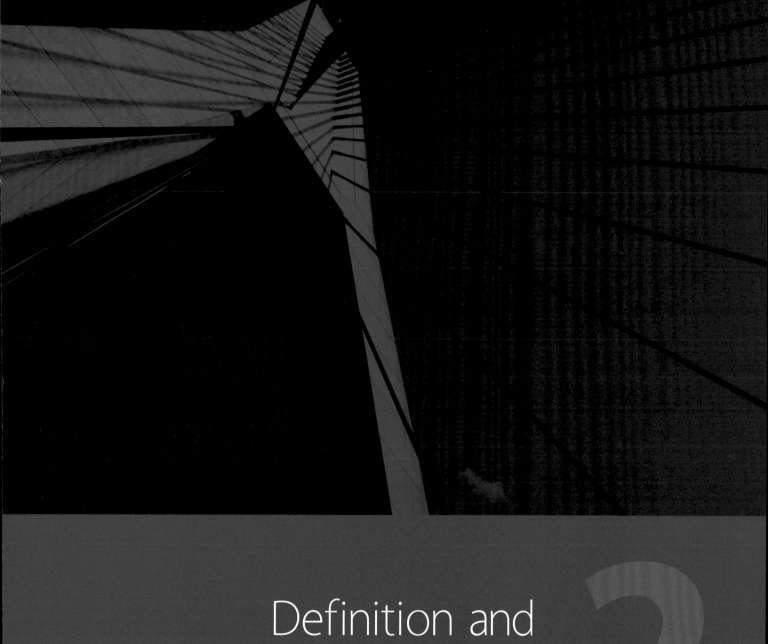

Definition and
context of project and
programme teams

2

2 Definition and context of project and programme teams

'A team is a small group of people with complementary skills committed to a common purpose and set of specific performance goals.' (Katzenbach and Smith, 1993)

'Team – a team is made up of two or more people working interdependently towards a common goal or shared reward.' (Project Management Body of Knowledge, Association for Project Management)

This chapter explains:

- How teams differ from groups
- How managing project teams is different from line management
- What the different motivating factors are for team members
- How the team leader is also affected by these different motivating factors
- What the three key team-leadership activities are in project and programme management.

2.1 TEAMS VERSUS GROUPS

Teams are different from groups in that each person within the team shares the same goal or purpose. Therefore, as the manager of a team, it is possible to give instructions, send messages or set standards that all members of the team will follow in broadly the same way. In a group, each individual would have to be persuaded to carry out the same activities as all of the other individuals. Therefore, managing people as a team creates efficiency benefits that cannot be gained within a group. Also within the team there is the idea of one plus one is greater than two – in other words, as team members work together they have

the power to create something greater than their own individual contribution.

2.2 TEAM MANAGEMENT VERSUS LEADERSHIP

At its core, team management is a form of leadership; however, it is undertaken at a more 'hands on' level than leadership. The latter addresses the direction of the work rather than the mechanics of completing the work. Team management is about achieving things through the motivation and coordination of groups of people who are tied together by a common aim. Leadership is about setting the direction that individuals must follow. Leadership asks people to pull in the same direction, whereas team management more actively 'pushes' them in that direction.

Team management for projects and programmes is different from leading other types of team because of the temporary nature of projects and programmes. There is usually a deadline by when the project must be completed, at which point the team will be disbanded. It is not always easy to put the energy into getting to know colleagues and how they work when they will not be around for very long.

Another important consideration is that a project team does not necessarily consist of the same people throughout the project lifecycle. Starting and initiating the project may involve a different set of people from those who actually end up delivering the work. Those delivering the work form a number of different teams as specialist suppliers join and leave the team as the work progresses. However, it is worth noting that although the team members at the end of the project lifecycle might all be different from those who first made up the project team, a completely new team has not formed each time. Instead, iterations or mutations of the team are developed, because the objectives, values and processes that the team adopts at the start usually remain the same throughout the lifetime of the team.

A skilled team leader will recognize that this is the best position to be in, because actually forming a brand new team each time someone leaves or joins would not deliver the project within the constraints of time and budget. Figure 2.1 shows an example of nine iterations of a project team during the project lifecycle; however, the number of iterations will vary with each project.

2.3 INDIVIDUAL GOALS AND OVERALL TEAM GOALS

Another consideration for the team leader is the way in which the team members in these different iterations react to each other, and their perception of the mission and goals of the team. For example, in the early stages of the lifecycle, team members are often internal members of staff, who have a shared organization, and potentially some shared history. The goal for the team is to debate the objectives of the project and come to an understanding of what is required.

Once the project is up and running, team members may be drawn from supplier companies, or freelance staff, as the work demands specialist skills. The team structure

Figure 2.1 Example of the different iterations of a project team during the project lifecycle

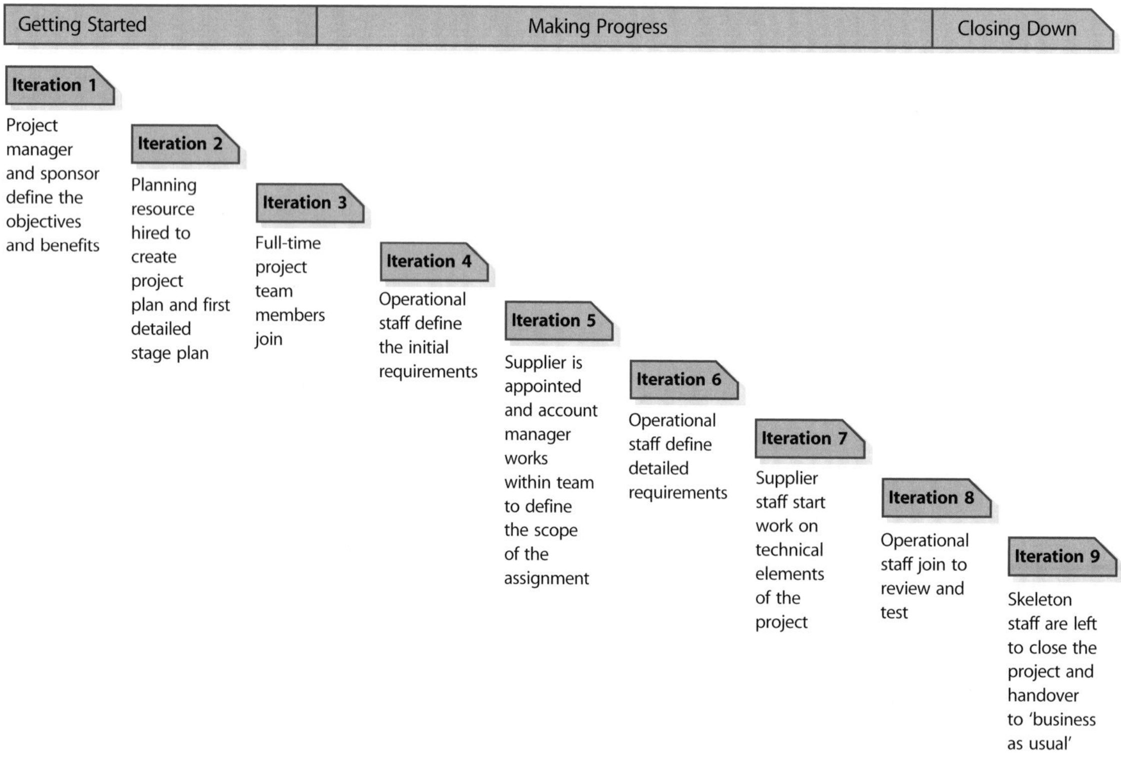

that has been built up can start to fragment, as these team members are more focused on the delivery of their specific piece of work than they are on the goals of the overall team. They may not work for the host organization, so they may not share the values of that organization, and because they are very aware of the short-term nature of the team they do not have the impetus to become involved in team-building activities.

When the project is coming to a close, the team starts to fragment again as the individual goal of each team member shifts to securing their future role, whether on this or on another project, or taking up another role within the host organization. At this point, the goal of the overall team has not changed, i.e. completion of the project, but what this means individually to each of the team members starts to become more important to them.

Unlike in 'business as usual' situations, team members may include freelance/contract staff, employees of the 'host' organization as project team members or operational staff who have to work alongside the project team, and

Figure 2.2 Interests of different team members

Freelance/contract staff

Positive
Wants successful project to build reputation and track record

Negative
Reviews job offer for other possible project opportunities that may be better paid, closer to home etc.

Employee who becomes a member of the project team

Positive
Wants successful project to build reputation and track record

Negative
Is concerned about becoming distant from the operational environment and the possible job opportunities and career path that are available

Employee who has to work alongside member of the project team

Positive
Wants successful operational environment to build reputation track record

Negative
Concerned that time taken away from operational duties will have a negative effect on their ability to carry out the 'day job'

Employees from supplier organizations

Positive
Wants successful project to build reputation and track record within supplier organization

Negative
Concerned that compromises that have to be made on the project will be an additional cost to the supplier and will impact negatively on how they are regarded by their boss

employees from supplier organizations. Each of these people will have their own loyalties, which will affect how much effort they will put into becoming an effective team member. Figure 2.2 shows the different interests that each team member may bring to the team, and whether they impact the team positively or negatively.

2.4 PERSONALITY AND PREFERENCES OF DIFFERENT TEAM MEMBERS

The ability to manage any team will be impacted by the values and behaviours that each team member displays. There are numerous models and profiling tools that can be used to outline the different personality types that team members display during the life of the project. However, whilst these are useful, they are generalizations, and the team leader has a responsibility to consider the specific motivation and values of each team member. The preferences for how each team member approaches their work, interacts with their colleagues and keeps people informed of progress, problems and changes is formed as a result of their personality, their experience and their personal goals. It is not possible for a team leader to know exactly what will motivate each team member, but there are a number of factors that can be considered when building and maintaining relationships.

Using lessons learned or stepping into the unknown

Some team members may be motivated by the opportunity to put right the things they felt could have been improved from the last project they were involved in. Therefore, they will look for similarities with previous work, and the freedom to undertake this work in the way that they now feel they 'know' works best.

However, other team members might find any reference to the past boring. They are motivated by change and

new opportunities and will therefore seek out chances to work in areas where the answers are not already known.

There are advantages to the improvements offered by the lessons learned; however, no two projects are the same. On the one hand there is the risk of trying to force the work into a similar shape to the last project when this is not appropriate; on the other hand, it is not always a good idea to ignore what has gone before, and a number of efficiencies can be gained from re-using plans, Risk Logs, etc. from previous projects.

Early adopters or those who need to be persuaded

Some team members hear an instruction and immediately start to plan how they will carry it out. They may not need to stop to consider if it is the right instruction. To them, it is a piece of work that they are skilled and experienced enough to do, so they just get on with it. Any further information takes time to listen to and just holds them back, when they are impatient to get on with the task. This means that they will not always listen to the details and can miss out on vital information, which they replace with their own assumptions.

Other team members need to be convinced that what they are being asked to do is the right thing. They may need reassurance that it is the correct piece of work for the project, or the reassurance they seek might be more personal, needing to know that they have the skills and experience to be successful. In this case, these team members can appear to doubt the word of the team leader, often questioning what they are being told several times before they become convinced. This can take time and cause friction, but it has the advantage of ensuring that all of the details are agreed before work commences.

Needing detailed instructions or outline tasks

Some team members prefer to be given their work with lots of instructions, and will check their understanding of these in a precise manner before feeling that they understand the task and are ready to commit to it. These team members often demonstrate close attention to detail in their own work, and therefore they seek this out from others. Failure to match this behaviour can lead to a very slow start to the work, as the team member will investigate and research on their own, until they discover the requisite amount of detail.

Others may prefer to be given the 'bigger picture', with very little detail about how the work should be conducted. This gives them the choice to decide on their own approach, and is important in how they interpret how they are viewed within the team. Often, these people will regard detailed instructions as a lack of trust in their ability to get the job done, so whilst the team leader feels they are being helpful in providing a detailed briefing, the team member is feeling insulted, believing their judgement to be in question.

Operating in the present or the future

Some team members will naturally concentrate on the future, and are motivated and interested in all of the activities that need to take place tomorrow, or next week or next month. This means that they may be very good at planning and looking ahead but they do not always give 100% concentration to the task that needs to be completed today.

Other team members may like to operate in the present, and cannot see past the task they are currently working on. They will finish this task to the required level of quality and be fully engaged in it, so they can be relied on to get the job done. However, they may find it more difficult to look ahead and see how their current work might be affected by things that need to be done in the future.

Motivated by the destination or the journey

Some team members are very focused on the end goal and what will be delivered to the organization as a result of their work or as a result of the project overall. Others, whilst cognizant of the end goal need to feel that the journey is also enjoyable. When motivating team members who focus on the destination, care must be taken to emphasize the need to follow all of the steps along the way, as this is a group that is likely to 'cut corners' to get where they are going as fast as possible. When planning their work, they are likely to provide high-level activities and their progress reports may include general statements about their achievements rather than detailed feedback on progress.

Those who are motivated by the journey will want sufficient time to undertake each task properly and will feel frustrated if they are moved through the work at a pace that feels uncomfortable for them. They may provide detailed plans and will enjoy talking through what they are going to do. Their detailed approach is useful for identifying interdependencies and risks, and mentoring more inexperienced colleagues.

The team leader is also impacted by these motivations and will need strong self-awareness to be able to understand how their motivation impacts on their understanding of each of the tasks in the Project Plan and the way in which these tasks are distributed to team members. For example, if a team leader has the following motivational preferences, these will impact on how they authorize work to team members and how they build relationships within the team:

- Stepping into the unknown
- Early adopters
- Outlining tasks
- Operating in the future
- The destination.

The team leader is motivated by change and new opportunities and is likely to be very enthusiastic at the start of a project, as the chance to seek out new ideas and new ways of working is high. Later in the project, this enthusiasm may reduce as the day-to-day project work takes on a repetitive edge, which has an effect on the amount of encouragement that this team leader offers their project team. As an early adopter, the team leader wants to jump straight into the project as quickly as possible. A preference for outline tasks means they will start work as soon as they feel they understand the 'big picture'. This means they are not particularly patient with team members who want to research the situation and familiarize themselves with the project information. Being motivated by the future inspires this team leader to concentrate more on what comes next rather than what is happening now. Team members may find it hard to report progress to this type of team leader unless they also provide details on the next set of activities that they have planned. Even though this person is managing the team, their preference of destination over journey means that they may not pay as much attention to procedures and processes as other team leaders. This gives the team members the freedom to establish their own approach to their work.

2.5 THE TEAM LEADER'S VALUES AND BEHAVIOUR

The first thing that a team leader must realize is what their own values and behaviours are. They must have a high degree of self-awareness so that they can clearly position their own approach along with the approach of each team member. Only by understanding what differences exist can the team leader hope to bridge those differences.

For example, if the team leader has issues with delegating work to others and is always the first in and the last out from the office every day, they need to understand what drives them to behave like this. Do they believe that they have the best possible skills and experience for carrying out the work? Are they trying to protect their team members from an even heavier workload by carrying as much of the burden themselves? In both cases, it might indicate that the team leader does not trust the competence and ability of the other team members.

If the team leader says to team members 'don't bring me problems, bring me solutions', does this mean that they want to keep their distance from the work? Does it mean that they have ultimate trust in their team members and see this attitude as a way of providing challenge and stretching the team to learn from their own mistakes?

One of the hardest things to remember is that everything that is said or written as a team leader will be scrutinized and interpreted by the team. They will look for how the team leader is 'really' feeling about the project, or their work. Therefore, the team leader has a responsibility to demonstrate emotional restraint, and ensure that all communications to the team, informal and formal, are framed as positively as possible.

2.6 LEADERSHIP ACTIVITIES REQUIRED IN A PROJECT

Team mission and direction

It is important to set out the team mission and direction as team members need clarity of its objectives and an understanding, even in general terms, of how these objectives might be achieved. The most effective teams have a strong sense of their purpose, organize their work around that purpose and plan and set goals in line with that purpose. Those involved in projects and programmes are responsible for delivering change. Therefore, the objectives are essential in setting the destination that the team must arrive at. After all, unless the team knows where it is going, it does not stand much chance of getting there.

The team leader has a responsibility for ensuring that the overall direction of the project is broken down into specific actions that must be taken, and these actions must be communicated to each team member. This is usually done via the delegation of specific work to each team member.

Team roles, responsibilities and processes

Team members need to have clear roles and responsibilities, so that they can not only understand the shape and context of their contribution but also understand how this relates to other team members. A team needs to have certain enabling processes in place for people to carry out their work together. These can be 'operating processes', which are usually linked to the standards and processes in existence across the organization, and 'ground rules', which include processes for dealing with conflict, protocol and business etiquette that sets the standard for how each team member must be treated.

The team leader will need to be aware of any conflicts between how the team operates and the procedures in place in other areas of the organization, or within supplier organizations, that have overall 'ownership and authority' over the team member.

Team relationships

Team relationships develop over time and depend on the creation of trust and respect between the team members. The team members must actively communicate amongst themselves and with other teams. To build trust and collaboration the team members need to work together, exchanging information, ideas and opinions so that a sense of values can be identified and shared.

It is the responsibility of the team leader to guide the team through these activities. This publication provides guidance and examples on how this might be achieved.

Effective team management in the project lifecycle

3

3 Effective team management in the project lifecycle

This chapter explains the connections between team management and the project lifecycle. Specifically it attempts to address the team development issues that arise during a project and introduces the various team interactions that can be applied to deal with them. To illustrate how team management is used throughout the lifecycle of a project, a case study has been used to bring to life the points being made. The team management challenges and solutions presented in this chapter are drawn from interviews with many people involved in project and/or programme team management. Therefore, the case study used throughout the chapter is based on a typical project whose characteristics are representative of a range of internal projects that are undertaken within organizations. The text is complemented by quotes from the interviewees, presented as 'real world experience'.

Case study: the 'Time Saver' project

A rapidly expanding consulting firm (Fast Consult) is currently experiencing growing pains. One of its key objectives is to streamline its processes in order to remain competitive. A programme of work has been initiated to review all the departments and processes to look for opportunities to increase efficiencies.

Based on feedback from the accounting department, a new and improved timekeeping system is urgently needed. In order to accurately bill clients, employees need a better way to track their time against each account they work on. The current method of staff members tracking their own hours on spreadsheets is disorganized and unproductive. The payroll unit is spending many hours deciphering employee spreadsheets in order to send out invoices. The official corporate directive resulting from this assessment requests that an automated, online tool be put in place.

The accounting director has signed on to be the sponsor, taking ownership of the project that will introduce an automated timekeeping tool within the next six to eight months. A project manager within the accounting department has also been appointed (Figure 3.1). Four internal team managers have been assigned to help with the project, coming from the IT, administration, consulting and accounting departments. An external team manager will join the team once the third-party supplier for the new system has been found. The sponsor has appointed three senior managers as the key decision-makers representing the consulting, accounting and IT departments. Two administration staff have also been added with project-support roles.

Figure 3.1 Management structure for the Time Saver project

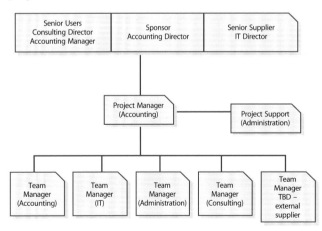

Therefore, there are two main teams for the 'Time Saver' project (Figure 3.2):

- The key decision-makers
  - One sponsor
  - Two senior users
  - One senior supplier.
- The project team
  - Project manager
  - Five team managers
  - Project support.

Figure 3.2 The two teams and sub-teams in the 'Time Saver' project

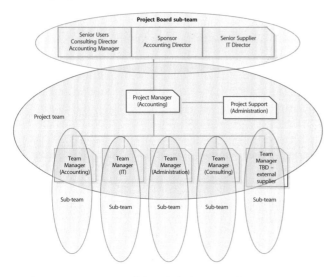

Each team manager will head their own sub-teams (Figure 3.2) in their departments, who will be required to undertake specialist work for the project.

This effort has been designed as a project, mainly because of its size, complexity and duration. However, if the effort had involved a strategic change within the organization where extensive coordination among multiple directorates would be required, then it could have been set up as a programme. In a programme environment, each division would require a separate project team to roll out the new system within their area, with business change

managers instilling the change within the operational units (Figure 3.3).

Figure 3.3 Example programme set-up

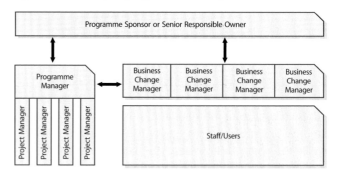

Regardless of the project or programme set-up, the team management challenges and complexities remain the same. Project and programme teams will be made of individuals from disparate groups who have not worked together before. At least one member will be from an external source, who may or may not be a virtual team member, depending on their location. The objectives for the effort are still quite vague and ambitious with the time constraints already defined. The following section focuses on the project team's development and interactions, but the principles discussed could easily be applied to the programme teams and sub-teams.

3.1 GETTING STARTED – STARTING THE PROJECT

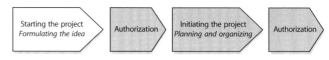

In the initial phase, a newly formed project team comes together to help confirm the need for the project by defining the project objectives, scope, approach and business justification.

Team mission and direction

Direction may be imposed on the team because the objectives of the project have been established as part of the initial project idea or the vision for the programme. However, there is still opportunity to explore what the chosen direction means to each team member. Often, the objectives of the project at this point are designed at a very high level and there is plenty of opportunity to build consensus with the team about what this will look like at the lower levels of detail. This gives team members an opportunity to contribute with their specialist knowledge, and an opportunity to start to find their own desired place within the team.

Case study: understanding the vision

The objective of the Time Saver project is to introduce an automated timekeeping tool, and there is plenty of opportunity for team members to share past experiences, their own understanding of what this will mean to the business, how best to approach the work and what some of the challenges are likely to be.

The responsibility of the team leader during this time is to ensure that everyone becomes involved, and that all contributions are treated with respect, even if they later prove to be unworkable. One way of achieving this is to hold a workshop, where the purpose is to go down to as low a level of detail as possible about what the project means to each team member. Using the structure offered by Product Based Planning or Work Breakdown Structures,

Figure 3.4 Initial project announcement

Use of 'our' shows that the Team Leader is involved in the project and has already taken some personal ownership of its outcome

This comment specifically addresses those who feel comfortable working from the perspective of how things have worked previously

This is a general point to everyone to reassure them that their contribution will be treated with respect and will be used as part of the project

Good morning, thanks for coming. The 'Time Saver' project is very exciting as it has the potential to make a substantial contribution to our competitiveness.

It has been agreed that a new time-keeping system will be implemented by us over the next 6–8 months, but no decisions have yet been taken on what this system will be. Part of our role here is to share our ideas and identify potential options for the way forward.

We have a lot of representatives from IT and Accounting here today, and I am hoping that we can learn many of the lessons associated with the implementation of the FIN1 system that we did last year.

However, we must also bear in mind that our market is changing, and that the ability to run sophisticated reports about time per employee and billing rates per customer must be designed to take account of future requirements and not just to meet the needs of today.

Please join me in working through the objectives for this project using the flipcharts around the room. The results of all the ideas shared here today will be sent out via email by the end of tomorrow.

Mentioning the decision that has already been taken reassures those who like an ordered world, whilst outlining the freedom for making decisions reassures those who like to be in control of their destiny

This comment specifically addresses those who need to feel they are stepping into the unknown the team manager can encourage team members to be as creative as they like, share their experiences with their colleagues, outline how they have seen similar work done in the past and show how different pieces of work link together.

Case study: addressing different motivational preferences

Some team members will be motivated by the opportunity to put into practice everything that they have learnt on previous projects. Others will be motivated by the opportunity to create something, so they enjoy the feeling of stepping into the unknown. The team leader cannot necessarily identify the preferences of individual team members at this early stage in the project. Even if they could, it is important to ensure that the purpose of the workshop is introduced in such a way that it appeals to everyone involved. Therefore, the team leader must ensure that their instructions address each preference.

As seen in Figure 3.4, different paragraphs of the initial project announcement address the different motivational preferences of the team members.

Team roles, responsibilities and processes

At this very early stage of a project, it is not always possible or desirable to appoint specific team members to specific roles. Until the objectives of the project are fully understood, the roles required and those most suitable for those roles may not be apparent. However, the team members are already starting to interact, so it is important to consider the processes and procedures that apply to this team. For example, basic rules on timekeeping, suitable attire and who should attend which meetings can be defined.

These procedures are an important factor in defining a team culture or environment. Whatever that environment turns out to be, understanding the rules gives each team member an opportunity to feel as if they belong. The team leader must define this culture, even if the ideas for it are provided by the team members themselves. A useful way to establish some of these ground rules is for the team leader to imagine they are absent for a period of time, perhaps on holiday for a couple of weeks. In this situation, how would the team leader want their team to behave? What things would the team leader expect to be done every day? What things must not be forgotten?

> **Real world experience**
>
> 'We need to agree the basics. Phones must be answered quickly, and people should sound interested to talk to whoever has rung them. Emails must be replied to promptly, even if it's just to say when the issue will be reviewed in detail.'
>
> 'Team meetings should take place whether I am there or not. People should still take responsibility for keeping each other up to date with what they are doing.'

Team relationships

At this point in the project lifecycle, the main relationships will be between each team member and the team leader. Therefore, the team leader has to take an active role in developing knowledge of each team member, and showing empathy for the way in which they approach their work. At the same time, the team leader has to be prepared to be open about their own values and approach to work, so that the team member has a basis on which to build a relationship. Relationships develop through the sharing of confidences.

Confidences need not be work related, and even getting to know how someone takes their coffee is a relationship building step. The team leader must be prepared to invest the time in these activities, a great deal of which is one-to-one with each team member. The time invested at this point is likely to go a long way to minimizing any misunderstandings later in the project lifecycle, and also makes the team a pleasant environment in which to operate. All the people interviewed for this publication pointed out how much time was required for this 'getting to know you' step, including after-hours socializing and the need to allow meetings to have a lot of 'socializing' time built into them, so that people can swap information and have the time for conversations which they often have at their desks. Even though it is recognized that a great deal of project communication will be via email, it is important to ensure that everyone knows the faces and the personalities behind the email accounts.

Real world experience

'Getting people together is very important. The downtime before the team meeting, when everyone gets a chance to chat over a cup of coffee, is sometimes more important than the meeting itself. It's where information is exchanged and relationships are built.'

'Most of the team building takes place by the coffee machine. It's where the day-to-day, almost meaningless chat happens about what people are doing at the weekend, or what they watched on TV last night. But it is not meaningless, it's how all relationships start – so every time I start a new project, my first job is to put a big tin of biscuits by the coffee machine and let the talking start.'

Case study: getting to know each other

In these early stages of the Time Saver project, the team leader should consider holding frequent team meetings, where a different team member is asked to 'host' the meeting each time. This gives each team member time to establish themselves as an individual, and their colleagues can see how they behave, how they organize themselves, and how they address issues and chair discussions. This is a good way for the team leader to start the process of building relationships between team members, and not always have the relationships flow through the team

leader. It is especially important as the team members come from four different departments within Fast Consult and may have different ways of approaching their work.

Real world experience

'The least effective team meeting is when we go through progress that has been made. Those who are not speaking get bored, as they are only really interested in talking about their bit, and it's too easy for others to criticize or start blaming each other if the progress is not as good as it could be. It is far better if we come together with a focus.'

3.2 GETTING STARTED – AUTHORIZATION

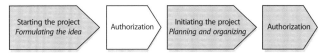

At the point of authorization for a project, the project team is waiting for the decision from the project sponsor, project board or sponsoring group on whether or not to proceed to the next step. If the decision-makers elect to take this first authorization decision in a meeting format, some team members along with the project manager may need to attend. The role of the team member would be to answer questions, especially technical or specialist questions from the findings discovered in starting the project.

In a programme, the process remains the same, although the team members involved may be representatives from the operational environment (business change managers) or project managers representing projects from the first tranche of the programme.

Team mission and direction

The mission for the project or programme team is to gain this authorization and move on to the detailed planning. This is a relatively short-term goal, but it is straightforward and easy to motivate the team around it.

Team roles, responsibilities and processes

Whilst formal roles may not yet have been appointed, authorization can identify those team members who are more likely to be called on to present to sponsors and senior managers. This might be as a result of seniority, past experience or specialist knowledge, but the team leader must ensure this additional responsibility is reflected in the job description for each impacted team member. This is also a useful opportunity to put in place procedures for designing and delivering presentations and communications to stakeholders outside the project team.

Team relationships

Identification of some team members as being responsible for senior-level communication can be a setback to any fledgling relationships by, in effect, creating two teams, one of which is perceived as having the confidence of the team leader to speak on behalf of the project and the other team not having this trust. By being clear and open about the criteria by which the 'communicators' have been chosen, the team leader can overcome this problem. They should also make it clear that once other team members meet the criteria, they will also have the opportunity to address meetings and represent the project, and that these sorts of activities are on a voluntary basis as many people have a dislike of public speaking. The team leader should also involve all team members in defining and creating the content of the presentation material so that all of the team members feel that the ideas explored in starting the project have been fairly represented.

3.3 GETTING STARTED – INITIATING THE PROJECT

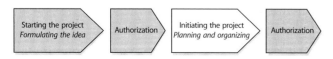

The focus during this stage of a project will be on defining, planning and organizing all of the work of the project. In order to understand, agree and complete this work, the team members must be able to work together, sharing their specialist knowledge, challenging each other's assumptions and agreeing the basis for estimating and scheduling. Additional resources may be added to help complete the required documentation. This means that new members are added to the team. Though the original team may be at the fulfilment stage of team development, the new members may not be. They are entering the team in the familiarization stage (see Appendix C). This may have an adverse effect on the existing team dynamics and cause the team as a whole to move backwards in the team development stages.

The team leader now needs to ensure that these new members are brought into the team quickly and that the old members accept them.

Team mission and direction

The mission for the project team is to complete the project within budget and timescale, to the required level of quality. The original team members explored what that meant to them during the starting of the project. However, once the project moves into initiation, other members may join the team, and will need to review what the objectives of the project mean for them, and how they see their contribution fitting into what has already been agreed.

If the team leader does not allow this review to take place, the team will become disjointed, as some team members may feel that the new members are 'moving in' on their specialist areas, and the new team members may feel there is conflict between their views of what the project should deliver and what has already been agreed.

Those team members who have been involved from the beginning will feel ownership over the project objectives, which have now been endorsed as part of the authorization of project start-up. This 'ownership' may make them unwilling to open up to new team members and may create an environment in which the original team members 'protect' the objectives and defend them against new thinking. The team leader needs to give careful thought to how new team members can be integrated into the team.

Integrating new team members

One way of integrating new team members is by using the buddy system. Each original team member takes responsibility for a new team member, explaining what has happened on the project so far and the background to the project. It is far harder to resent someone or fail to communicate with them if the team member has been asked to be responsible for their integration. This is a simple and effective way of reducing team conflict.

Another solution is to expand the understanding of the project work and those whom it impacts, so that 'old' and 'new' team members develop new understanding about the project rather than just going over old ground. This can be done in a number of iterations, with individual or small groups of team members taking responsibility for a specific part of the project. At the end of each iteration, the group should come together and discuss their findings and their views as a team, before splitting off once more,

Figure 3.5 Understanding the project – iteration one

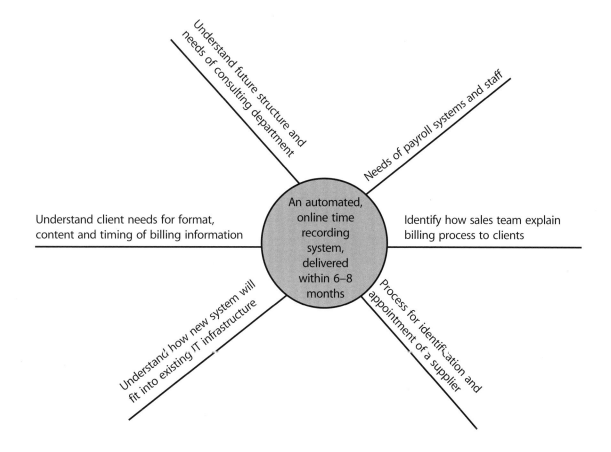

sometimes into different small teams, to increase the interaction between all of the team members.

Case study: expanding the understanding of the project

On the Time Saver project, the first two iterations may look like the iterations shown in Figures 3.5 and 3.6.

Team roles, responsibilities and processes

The team leader has to identify the skills needed for the planning, estimating and scheduling work that is needed to complete the project or programme plan. Other resources will need a high degree of interpersonal skills in order to complete the requirements definition with the users who are impacted by the project. Once the analysis

Figure 3.6 Understanding the project – iteration two

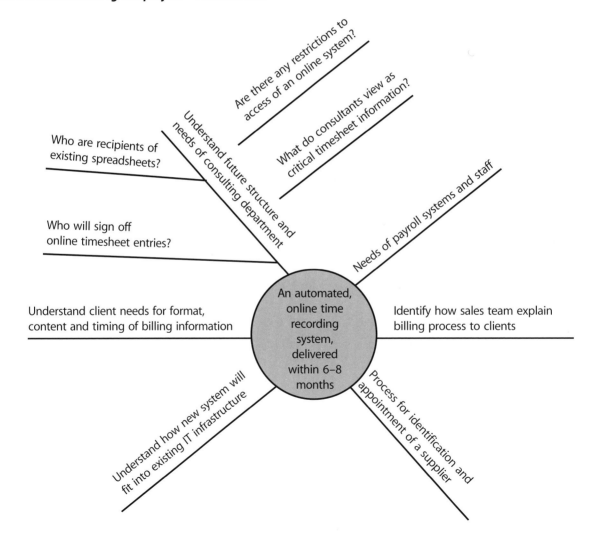

Are there any restrictions to access of an online system?

What do consultants view as critical timesheet information?

Understand future structure and needs of consulting department

Who are recipients of existing spreadsheets?

Who will sign off online timesheet entries?

Needs of payroll systems and staff

Understand client needs for format, content and timing of billing information

Identify how sales team explain billing process to clients

An automated, online time recording system, delivered within 6–8 months

Understand how new system will fit into existing IT infrastructure

Process for identification and appointment of a supplier

of resources has been carried out, the team leader can start to map the available resources against the roles required and form an opinion of how the team should look.

Case study: mapping roles to the right people

The Time Saver project team leader should consider the different motivating factors for each team member, and give some of the detailed planning tasks to those who are motivated by the journey or who like to receive detailed instructions rather than an outline of the bigger picture. For risk analysis tasks, the leader should involve those members who are keen to apply lessons learned and those who need to be persuaded about the value of a piece of work.

Whilst it is important for the team leader to have this structure, the structure must remain sufficiently flexible to take into account the interests and needs of the team members. For example, a team member might know a lot about the outputs being created by the project and so they are a natural choice to lead the requirements gathering with the users. However, they may have a strong desire to take a much greater role in the planning and scheduling activities. In this case, the team leader will need to reach a compromise agreement, whereby that team member perhaps takes part in some aspects of requirements gathering but is not the sole resource. Their knowledge and expertise are just as valuable in scheduling activities which take into account all of the interdependencies, of which they may have a good understanding.

One-to-one meetings

The team leader should meet individually with each team member to review a draft set of responsibilities, then discuss and agree them. This may be the first one-to-one meeting between the team leader and the team member, so sufficient time should be scheduled for there to be a real discussion and an opportunity to clarify any misunderstandings or misconceptions about the role. The team member will form a strong opinion about how

the team leader works, which will affect their working relationship during the life of the project. Therefore, the team leader needs to take basic steps to ensure that this meeting goes as well as possible, such as:

- Turn up on time
- Ensure there is sufficient privacy for discussion to take place
- Come well prepared, with an outline of all the team roles, a description of this role and how it fits into the other roles
- Ensure that any background information about the team member, which has influenced the decision on which role they will take, is available to discuss, in case the team member feels that they have been given an inappropriate role
- Take this opportunity to establish any important ground rules about how team members are to behave.

Real world experience

'I think it is important to start as we mean to go on. I have three basic rules that I want every team member to follow, and I make this clear as early in the project as possible:

- Turn up on time – it's rude to keep others waiting. No-one is so important that they cannot be on time for a meeting, and that includes me.
- Come prepared – never show up to a meeting without the relevant papers or a notepad. It is not possible to remember everything that is happening, so write it down.
- Don't email unless the person you want to speak to is out. Pick up the phone and talk.'

Team relationships

Often it is not possible to select the team members for a project. Other factors such as availability and the need for certain technical skills will determine who becomes a member of the team. This is particularly true if the project has employed supplier organizations, as they will supply the resources that they think best fit the job, and that are available for the duration of the project.

Case study: helping to build relationships

'Outsiders' are joining the Time Saver team in the form of staff from an external supplier organization. The team leader should ensure that this is communicated in a positive way, because the communication may determine the team atmosphere into which these new members are welcomed.

The team leader can increase the effectiveness of this announcement by ensuring it addresses the different motivational preferences of the different team members (Figure 3.7). Each paragraph of the announcement in the figure addresses different motivational preferences, thus covering all the team members. By addressing several different motivational preferences, the team leader

does not have to worry about analysing who has what preference – each team member will be motivated by the announcement as at least a part of it was communicated in the way they most prefer.

Factors influencing relationships

It is essential for the team leader to develop relationships with each team member and value them for who they are, rather than holding them responsible for not being what the team leader wanted.

The easiest way to achieve this is to understand the values and behaviours that each team member has. Their values drive the things that they do, and the way in which they do them. Their behaviours are the way in which they relate to others and undertake their work.

It is difficult for anyone to clearly articulate the values that drive their behaviour. These are often deep within

Figure 3.7 Announcement by team leader

1 For those team members who need to be persuaded, include details of the other suppliers who were evaluated, the evaluation criteria and the reasons why they were not selected

3 For those motivated by lessons learned in the past, include reference to previous implementations and procedures projects and highlight key differences or improvements

Following the earlier procurement process, A1B1 systems has been appointed as our supplier for the Time Saver system **1**

A1B1 has developed a number of similar systems and is confident it can meet our aggressive deadlines **2**

The A1B1 system will give us the opportunity to build new interfaces between our existing systems, and make significant changes to the billing processes currently in use **3**

2 For those motivated by the journey, include information on what skills and information will be learnt along the way, and describe some of the interim products that will be created as a result of the system implementation. This will also answer the needs of those who prefer greater detail than just a 'big picture'

the subconscious, although they can be brought out by tapping into these subconscious thoughts. Two well-regarded techniques for getting to understand values and beliefs are the use of metaphors and story telling.

Metaphors are a substitute for the subject being discussed. For example, when discussing how the team is performing it is common to use sporting or military metaphors to describe the situation without having to be specific about the team members involved. A team leader might decide to compare the project to a football team, aligning the completion of a particular task with the need to score a goal. Alternatively, if the team is about to face a significant challenge, perhaps meeting an aggressive deadline, the team leader might use a metaphor about an army winning a battle.

By asking team members to describe how they see a situation by using a metaphor, a great deal of information can be gained about the importance that a team member places on the situation, whether they subconsciously see it as positive or negative for the project and whether they are hopeful or pessimistic for the chances of success. For example, if a team member describes the handover activities to the operating staff as 'swimming against the tide', this implies that the tide is a very strong force, and that swimming against it feels pointless and is very tiring. It implies that the team member sees the operating staff as having greater power than the project team. Before any further progress can be made on the handover activities, the amount of authority that the project team has for getting operating staff to take part in briefings and attend training sessions will need to be explored.

Stories, however simple, are also a great way of getting messages across in a compelling way. After all, everyone likes to hear a story

Case study: establishing the team environment

The team leader of the Time Saver project needs to set out the environment that they believe should operate within the team. They can do this by establishing lots of rules, but it is more effective if they use a story. For example, to convey to all team members that they should work together and be helpful towards each other, the team leader could tell the following story:

'I was once working on a project where all of the team members had to do a lot of travelling, staying in hotels during the week and only getting home at weekends. It was great for the first few weeks, as it was exciting to stay in nice hotels and go out for dinner and get to know my colleagues. After a few weeks, I started to feel tired, and I was missing my family. Silly things started to annoy me, like not being able to get up and make a cup of coffee without ringing room service, not being able to take a bath because the hotel room only had showers. What I really appreciated during this time was that I got to know my colleagues as friends, and we were all able to laugh at the things that were irritating us, and when one of us was feeling low, the others would rally round and help out. One guy needed to leave halfway through the week because his daughter was in the school play, and another colleague needed to come in late on the Monday because she was spending the weekend with her parents. We made sure their work was covered, because we always knew it could be one of us the next week.'

3.4 GETTING STARTED – AUTHORIZATION

This point in the lifecycle represents the second key decision made on a project without the team having formally started the specialist work. Some or all of the team members will have gone through the authorization process before, so their anxiety about the decision may be less than before. However, usually the project team members have been performing at a high level as a team to create the initiation documentation.

Therefore, there may be feelings of loss and grief if the second decision is to not authorize continuation. Just the anticipation of the decision possibly being negative can bring on these feelings of anxiety. The project manager (team leader) will need to reassure the team during this step.

Team mission and direction

The mission for the project team is to gain the authorization for the plans, estimates, resource requirements and schedule, which will allow the team to start the specialist work. The authorization is a clear focus for the team but the team leader should take this opportunity to clarify what this authorization means to each team member. Ask them to consider what they see as the purpose of the project and clarify why they think the organization is willing to undertake this work.

Case study: exploring the team's commitment to the project

The Time Saver project team has learnt a great deal about the project whilst undertaking the detailed planning. However, this information will have been interpreted differently by each team member, and a deeper understanding of the purpose and goals of the team can be developed by sharing these views. For example, the

problems experienced by the accounting department using the current timesheets will affect how that team member views the project. This team member is very positive as they can see how easy it will be to bill clients accurately once the Time Saver system goes live. The secondee from the consulting department is feeling very negative as they are beginning to realize how much the existing working practices will have to change. The team leader decides to generate a discussion on the answers to the questions shown in Figure 3.8, which have been selected to draw out feelings and opinions about the winners and losers that will result from the project.

Figure 3.8 Project impact assessment questions

Workload
Who has the least work to do re timesheets in each department? Who has the most work to do?

Responsibilities	**Relationships**
Who reviews timesheets? Who authorizes timesheets?	Who talks to whom? Who knows the most about the processes? Who knows the least?

By asking the questions shown in Figure 3.8, the team leader can generate a useful discussion about where the team sympathy lies, which team members feel naturally supportive of particular areas of the organization and why. Sharing this with all team members widens the understanding of the impact of what the team is about to do, and strengthens individual commitment to these actions.

Team roles, responsibilities and processes

Although the decision is being taken by the sponsoring group, giving team members a role during this time can avoid lack of energy and motivation within the team:

- For those who have a preference for being convinced, involve them in communicating the results of the authorization meeting to other stakeholders as this will help them to appreciate the reasons behind the project and its importance to the achievement of the strategic direction of the organization.
- For those who have a preference for receiving detailed instructions, ask them to develop the tasks from the plan into detailed work packages, for themselves and other team members. Their attention to detail and the ability to break the tasks into small steps will be helpful in creating a format that can be used when preparing the work at the end of each stage.
- For those who are motivated by the destination, get them involved in communicating what this is to other stakeholders.
- For those motivated by the journey, partner them with those responsible for creating the work packages for the next stage of the project so that they can develop an idea of the activities that will be needed.
- For those motivated by using the lessons learned from previous projects, ensure they become involved in identifying what needs to be reviewed, and what should be asked at each review. They can base this on the things that went wrong last time.

Team relationships

During the pressures of initiation, the team should have started to gel, so this is an excellent time for the team leader to encourage the development of relationships between the team members. Whilst the involvement of the team leader is essential in creating and maintaining the team environment, the ability of the team to function creatively and with responsibility for the work will be restricted if the team leader has to be a part of every team relationship. The team leader has to be confident enough to make the team work as a team and not as a hierarchical structure.

> **Real world experience**
>
> 'I have to manage large teams of consultants on projects but I don't have the time to spend on them individually. My way of coping is to form them into different problem-solving units so that they have responsibility for more than just their own work. To get things sorted they have to work together as "mini" teams, which increases the interaction between them and stops them all looking at me as the only one who might have the answer.'

As the team grows, the team leader will not be able to maintain close relationships with every team member, and a natural process of accepting responsibility by those team members best placed to do so must take place. The team leader must foster these relationships and encourage the development of mini-teams through the careful delegation of work to different parts of the team, who will naturally start to develop working relationships with their colleagues to get the job done. The eventual pattern of communication is a web, in which different team members can work with other team members without this being identified, defined and controlled by the team leader.

3.5 MAKING PROGRESS – DAY-TO-DAY CONTROL

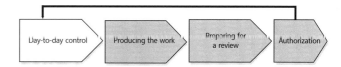

During this phase of a project, the stage plan will be used to allocate work by the team leader to individual team members.

Team mission and direction

At the start of each stage, the team leader should re-focus the team on its objectives, and relating how these more detailed objectives contribute to the project as a whole. This sets the context for the current stage of the project.

Case study: re-focusing on the project objectives

As the re-focusing exercise is a general message to all team members, the team leader should construct an explanation that addresses the different motivational preferences of each team member (Figure 3.9).

Aligning approaches to work with objectives and policies

The team leader not only needs to ensure that work that takes place will deliver the required outputs for the project but they must also ensure that the approach taken by the different team members acting as specialists in their own field is aligned to organizational policies and procedures.

Case study: implications for the Time Saver project team

On the Time Saver project, the team member responsible for gathering the user requirements from the payroll department expects to conduct process analysis and produce process flow diagrams of what currently happens in the department, create new process flows for what will happen after the time recording system is implemented

Figure 3.9 Project announcement

For those who need to be persuaded, include details of the other options considered, e.g. an online guide, help cards or an e-learning system

There needs to be a new process guide for the consultants so that they have a reference for using the Time Saver system ①

It needs to be short and user-friendly, and must be distributed to them before training starts in two months' time ②

We should try and make it look 'fun and interesting', but we have to keep the production costs low so let's make sure we get a good deal from our printing suppliers ③

For those who like detail, explain what 'short' and 'user-friendly' mean as both are open to interpretation

Again, for those who like using lessons from the past, reference can be made to the type of printing deal that has been created in the past. For those who like detail, explain what 'fun and interesting' means, as it is open to interpretation and document the gap between the two as the first step in requirements gathering.

Another team member will gather requirements from the consulting department by holding focus groups and one-to-one interviews.

To ensure consistency of the deliverables from the project the team leader and team members will have to agree what is needed from the requirements phase and how the different approaches contribute to this. The team members should be encouraged to explain why they want to approach the work in this way. For example, the team member wishing to conduct interviews may have had success with this technique in the past and is very confident of their ability to ascertain the required information in this way. The team member who wishes to conduct gap analysis was taught this technique by her previous organization and strongly believes this is the 'correct' way to gather requirements. The team leader recognizes that to impose one method will create a situation of 'winner' versus 'loser', which will negatively impact on team environment.

The different methods are associated with successful outcomes in the eyes of the team members, and to use a different method from the one they are familiar with may affect their confidence and the time it takes them to get the job done. The team leader also has to consider the formal and informal procedures that operate within Fast Consult as departmental heads may be unwilling to have their processes formally analysed or their staff interviewed. In Fast Consult, staff interviews only take place as part of performance appraisals, so holding interviews would not be suitable as a technique on this project.

Whatever decision is taken, the team leader should consider involving the team as a whole and not just those team members who are immediately affected, as the discussion and explanation will help to build the long-term procedures for the team, and provide a framework for handling other conflicts in the future.

The way in which the decision is received will be impacted by the way in which the team members are motivated (Figures 3.10 and 3.11). If the 'analyst' is motivated by the journey and not just the destination, and needs to be convinced rather than being an early adopter, then the team leader will need to put more effort into explaining the reasoning and reassuring them that the steps taken will work. If the 'interviewer' is motivated by the destination and is an early adopter, they will want a quick decision and the chance to get on with the work. Too much discussion may frustrate them, as they are motivated by what they achieve and not by how they achieve it.

Figure 3.10 Convincing the slow adopter why a particular method is to be followed in the project

Figure 3.11 Informing the early adopter why a particular method is to be followed in the project

Team roles, responsibilities and processes

The overall mission for the team during this part of the project is the creation of the required deliverables. However, this goal needs to be divided into individual responsibilities for each team member. Wherever possible, this allocation of roles will be based on an understanding and a desire to use the technical and interpersonal skills of the team member. However, whilst this is likely to be true for the majority of roles, there will be some activities that a team member is asked to perform that run counter to their view of their position in the team. The team leader needs to understand the perception that the team member has about their place in the team, and what their own strengths and weaknesses are. This might be a very different picture from that held by the team leader.

Before assigning roles, the team leader needs to get to know the team member as much as time pressures will allow. Sometimes it can be as simple as an explanation from the team leader about why they think that resource is best placed for that role. For example, the team leader has spotted a particular skill that the team member has and can explain how that skill relates to what needs to be done. At

other times, the team member may need more proof and encouragement that they have the skills to work in that particular context.

Case study: assigning responsibility skilfully

A team member in a previous stage has shown strong negotiating skills when keeping the supplier organization on track, and the Time Saver team leader wishes to use them in this stage to manage another supplier. If the team member is an early adopter, the team leader knows that giving some praise will be sufficient for the team member to undertake the role. But if the team member needs more convincing, the team leader may need to spend time giving examples of when they have seen the team member demonstrating this skill and outlining why they thought it achieved results. The team member may not have realized how strong their negotiating skills are, so the team leader will need to explain that the compromise they reached ensured that a particular component was delivered on time. The team member showed confidence in brokering this deal, understood the priorities for the organization in meeting the deadline, and investigated how much funding was available in the budget before making any promises.

Team relationships

Motivating individual team members is an essential role of leading the team. To be successful, it must be undertaken one-to-one, in quiet and uninterrupted surroundings, with sufficient time for a two-way exchange of views.

Although everyone will have a different way of addressing their team, and will use different words and phrases, there is a useful structure that can be applied to these meetings to ensure that motivation is achieved:

- Present – review what is happening now and identify areas where there are problems, and draw out from the identification of the problems any learning points that the team member would find valuable

- Past – examine the past behaviour and work of this specific team member, and identify past successes and similarities between the current problems and problems that they successfully overcame in the past
- Future – using the examples gathered in the present and the past, discuss how the current piece of work will be successfully completed.

For example, if a team member is finding their workload difficult to manage, the team leader would discuss the difficulties they are experiencing such as working late, working weekends, not being able to finish work to the right level of detail, feeling underprepared when attending meetings etc. The team leader then has to establish with the team member any patterns that they have identified which are particularly relevant to this overwork such as late delivery of work from other team members or overambitious estimating of the time or resources required. If the team leader can improve any of these technical issues, then they must do so.

The team leader should then turn their attention to the past, and ask the team member about any other examples of this sort of pressure that they have experienced, and what helped them overcome it. The team member must be encouraged to really think through how they successfully overcame these past pressures, to reinforce the point that they have the capacity to deliver the work, and that they will be successful.

The team leader should then move onto the future, discussing how things will look and feel once this particular piece of work has been completed. The team member should be encouraged to visualize this so that they see their future success.

Getting work under way in a programme requires the team leader to ensure that the goals of each project team do not conflict. In order to undertake team management in this dispersed environment, the team leader should concentrate on building the linkages between the

different teams (Figure 3.12). These teams can then use these relationships to exchange information and align the approach to quality, risk and change management across their project.

Figure 3.12 Ensuring linkage between the various teams in a programme

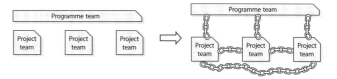

Building linkages requires an environment of inclusion so that projects do not act independently of all of the other projects and initiatives that form the programme. For example, the team leader hosts regular project briefings where one project team takes the lead in sharing their progress, challenges and solutions with the others. Project managers from one project are encouraged to attend meetings run by other projects when common areas of interest are being discussed, e.g. how to approach requirements gathering, what infrastructure will be needed for a test environment and what rules apply to the scheduling of user training.

3.6 MAKING PROGRESS – PRODUCING THE WORK

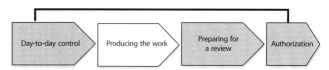

In this part of the project lifecycle, individual team members are given specific pieces of work by the team leader. Effort is usually focused on the technical aspects of getting the work done, and the team environment can suffer as team members become more insular as they concentrate on their own work.

Team mission and direction

Tasks delegated to team members or sub-teams are usually shorter in timeframe and more concentrated on specialist skills. Therefore, at this point in the project lifecycle, the goal becomes the successful completion of a specific piece of work, delivered on time, on budget and to the required level of quality. The team leader needs to ensure that the goal is clearly documented and agreed with the relevant team member.

The team leader can provide essential context for the piece of work, as they see how each piece fits into the bigger picture at the project, programme and organizational level. They should take time to explain the context, as it is vital motivation, especially if the work is unappealing, not challenging, repetitive or difficult to execute. They need to ensure that all team members are given a similar level of detail as team unity can be destroyed if certain team members are regarded as well informed and 'in the loop' and others are not.

The team leader needs to create their own method for briefing team members that takes into account their need for information and the additional insight that the team leader can bring. This includes sharing the views of other parts of the organization that a particular team member may not interact with, or giving a market-wide perspective to an issue that the team member is looking at solely from within the organization.

Case study: briefing team members

The Time Saver team leader uses the following factors as an agenda for providing contextual information to individual team members:

- Political factors – the team leader explains why certain managers are in favour or against the project. For example, timekeeping may be a contentious issue that is heavily resisted by the consultants because they see it as a method to monitor their levels of activity, with the implication that they will need to increase their billable hours.

- Financial factors – the team leader explains the impact of the project in terms of financial costs and benefits. Where will benefits be realized and where will ongoing costs be assigned once the project goes live? The payroll department will make significant savings, as it will no longer need to resource the manual entry of spreadsheet data but the consulting department will have to meet the running costs once the system becomes operational.

- Market factors – the team leader explains where the successful delivery of the project will place the organization in respect of its competitors or show how it is likely to be regarded by its customer base. The Time Saver project implements a system that many other consulting firms are already using, so this is essential to ensure the organization does not fall any further behind. The customers are in favour of the system as it provides them with the detailed breakdown of their bills that their own accounting systems are now demanding.

> **Real world experience**
>
> 'My team manager is really involved with us. She always seems to know what everyone is up to, and she gives us extra help by passing on her views and knowledge about who we are meeting with, the history or their career so we can see where they might be coming from. She seems to know everyone and she connects the dots so even though she is the manager, she is totally involved.'

Team roles, responsibilities and processes

As part of establishing the responsibilities for each team member, the team leader must ensure that the team member feels ownership over their role and its contribution to the project. This means that the team member must not be given responsibilities that are outside their ability to influence. For example, do not ask them to ensure that the users 'love' the timekeeping system. It is not in the control of the team member to ensure that the users 'love' or even 'like' the system. However, they can own the responsibility 'this is the best timekeeping system you have ever developed' because it is in their power to produce their best possible work.

In order to confirm the understanding of their responsibilities, the team member must identify the criteria by which they will know when they have met them. For example, the best system they have ever developed might be evidenced by the fact that it passes testing without any errors being discovered.

Team relationships

The environment that the team operates within can be affected by the behaviour of just one team member. If someone is unhappy with any aspect of the project, then the team leader must proactively investigate the issues that are causing this unhappiness. In some cases, the unhappy team member represents the views of all team members. In other cases, they are the only one with a negative view, which can be neutralized when they realize that others do not feel the same way.

Case study: dealing with a dissatisfied team member

The Time Saver project is entering the testing phase, and one team member is moaning about the lack of testing facilities. The team leader should investigate to find out if this is a genuine concern, or if the team member is masking unhappiness that might be rooted in exhaustion (the project has kept the team very busy for the last few months), a lack of understanding of what testing will involve or simply passing on the complaints from the operational staff who may not wish to get involved in the testing.

Dealing with negativity within the team

Once the underlying cause is discovered, the team leader must take action. Any proactive stance neutralizes the moaning, even if the action is to generate humour over something that cannot be changed. Laughing at the number of workstations available for system testing, joking that everyone is going to have to work in shifts through the night, or pair up and each have one hand on the keyboard can be good at releasing the tension.

If the unhappiness is team wide, then the team leader needs to hold a workshop or a short session within a team meeting to clarify what all of the issues are. It is no good fixing one area of concern if the team immediately turns its attention to another area of unhappiness.

The team leader will need to address this session in a very open manner, reassuring everyone that they recognize that there are concerns, and emphasizing how keen they are to fix them. Those who are motivated by early adoption are likely to jump right in, but others might need some convincing. The way to convince them is to highlight times when the team has hit problems before, outline what those problems were and remind the team members how they were overcome. This also inspires those motivated by lessons learned, and if the team leader comments on how fresh solutions will be required this time, it will assist those with a preference for stepping into the unknown.

Once all of the points have been gathered, the team leader should categorize them, so that the team members can see how many of the points are actually about similar issues. It is possible that the team leader can use this activity to highlight that whilst there are a lot of issues, they originate from only a couple of sources, and therefore that is where action should be directed. Another benefit of categorizing the issues is to recognize which ones are within the control of the project team, and which are imposed on them. Therefore, the team will not waste energy fighting against things that cannot be changed.

Case study: Problem identification and problem-solving

Figure 3.13 shows how the Time Saver team leader has categorized the issues under three headings.

Now that the items have been categorized, the team leader calls for a coffee break and ensures there is some social interaction between the team members and the team leader. However, they do not cut the session too short. People like to talk to each other during the break, and many of these conversations will be pertinent to the session:

■ Reassuring each other that they agreed with the points raised, and thanking their colleagues for raising them (which develops team unity)
■ Discussing the points and coming up with possible solutions.

The break is needed to move the session between its two forms – problem identification and problem-solving. Once back from the break, the team leader should generate an environment where the energy is directed at overcoming the issues that the group can control, addressing those issues that the team can influence and accepting those conditions that are imposed upon the team.

As a result of the workshop, the Time Saver team leader appoints one team member to be responsible for liaison with the consultants, and one team member to be responsible for liaison with the payroll staff, to more powerfully represent the priorities and concerns of the project. The team leader takes responsibility for the delay caused by the supplier and considers ideas for scheduling other project work for the weekends to overcome the conditions imposed by the availability of the training suite and overtime payments.

Figure 3.13 Project concerns

In control
• We do not have the rates for all of the consultants
• The supplier has still not provided the test data, which is delaying testing and training

Able to influence
• The consultants do not attend project briefings
• The system relies on data entry by payroll staff, which is slow

Imposed
• Training on the system is not allowed to take place at the weekend
• Payroll staff do not work after 5pm

3.7 MAKING PROGRESS – PREPARING FOR A REVIEW

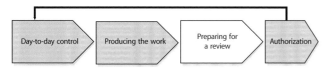

At this point, a project team will be nearing the end of the current stage and will need to review progress to date and prepare a plan for the next stage of the project. In programme terms, the progress of any transition activities and the realization of any benefits should also be reviewed. This is an opportunity to ask questions about how the group is performing as a team, and to identify any improvements that can be made at an individual and at a team level.

Team mission and direction

The team needs to focus on ensuring that all the work for this stage of the project is completed, quality reviewed and properly documented. The achievements of this stage must be taken into account when planning the next stage. Some of the team members will find a period of review easier than others. Those motivated by the destination or the future will find it harder to engage at this point in the project lifecycle and as this runs counter to their motivations, the team leader may need to take an active role in demonstrating how tidying up everything ready for an authorization helps ensure the ultimate delivery of the project.

Case study: preparing for a review

The Time Saver team leader has asked the team members to create presentations for stakeholders showing how the achievements to date indicate that the project is on target for success. This reinforces the message to the whole team, as well as providing a valuable update for stakeholders. As shown in Figure 3.14, the presentation starts from stage 3, as this is the stage that is just finishing, and shows how the work of stages 1, 2 and 3 have culminated in a system now ready for testing. Stage 4 illustrates how this testing work has been scheduled to take place, and how it is the last step before stage 5, when the project will be completed.

Team roles, responsibilities and processes

The procedures for completing a stage and preparing for reviews will be drawn from the values already established by the team leader. For example, if team members have been allowed to release products to the users before they were completed or reviewed during the production stage,

Figure 3.14 Project review

Stage 3	**Stage 4**	**Project completion**
 	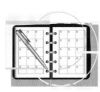	
System is now installed ready for testing	Test schedule will be created and users will join with project team for testing and quality review activities	System will be loaded onto the laptops for use by the consultants

they are going to try to cut the same corners at the end of the stage. Alternatively, if the team leader has implied that being on time is not as important as getting things right, then this attitude is likely to be applied to the end of the stage, with unexpected delays making it difficult to schedule a review.

The team leader should review how team members behave during this hiatus between stages to understand the informal team culture that has developed. Culture is about how things get done. It is much deeper than the formal organizational procedures, and is linked directly to the values and priorities that each team member has. If the team leader notices any distance between what they want to happen and what is actually happening, they must step in and reframe the situation.

Case study: implications for the Time Saver project

The team has developed an arrogant attitude, where they feel they know everything there is to know about automated timekeeping systems. Therefore, when a member of the payroll staff notifies the team that the format of the information will not work with one of the finance systems, the team is quick to dismiss the comment as a 'another complaint from Payroll'. This is showing

disrespect for the operational staff, and indicates that the team has become very inward focused, concentrating only on its collective views, and working hard to repel any information from outside the project team (Figure 3.15). Those outside the project team are being regarded as the 'enemies' of the project, the people who come up with reasons why the project will not be successful. The team leader needs to recognize that whilst it is important to have team unity, in this case the situation has gone too far.

The team leader will need to take the lead in reframing how those outside the project can be helpful to the project, and identify concrete examples where their knowledge will save time, prevent unnecessary changes in project scope and identify interdependencies between products that will make the design of the overall deliverable more robust and a better-quality product. It is unlikely that explaining how this will reduce costs will be particularly appealing to the team. This is because what they are really defending is their specialist knowledge and expertise – a culture of 'I know best' that has spread to all of the team members. Therefore, the team leader must answer this with an explanation of how 'outsiders' can provide information that only the 'specialist' team member really knows how to use. In other words, the

Figure 3.15 Negative and positive team unity

Positive team unity

Project team willingly accepts information from all sources and compares it against its specialist knowledge before deciding whether to include it in the approach to the project

Negative team unity

Project team rejects information from sources outside of the team as the team members believe their specialist knowledge is superior to any other information

team leader is to some extent playing to the vanity of the team members.

Team relationships

The team environment must be carefully managed when preparing for a review, so as to ensure that team members do not focus solely on the progress of their individual achievements and therefore become more insular and less of a team.

The team leader must actively review progress and step in to ensure team members are supporting each other to finish all of the work of the production stage. The message needs to be that the team will be evaluated on its total set of deliverables and not on any one piece of work. The team leader has to steer a course between those who want to wrap up the stage as quickly as possible and move onto the next stage, and those who want to continue perfecting the deliverables from this stage. The team leader can usefully partner team members with these different preferences to increase the pace of the work whilst maintaining the focus on quality.

The ability to motivate team members to conduct a review relies on the strength of the links between the review and the overall purpose of the team. The team leader should focus everyone back on the common goals of the team, after a period of specialist work when some team members may have broken away from the team. Team members should be asked to identify the contribution that this period of review is making to the successful delivery of the project, rather than the team leader lecturing them on this subject. They are more likely to own the outcomes and believe in them if they discover them for themselves, although the team leader should lead the discovery of this.

3.8 MAKING PROGRESS – AUTHORIZATION

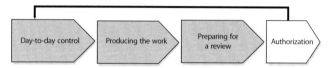

Team mission and direction

At the end of each stage, the team leader should ensure that all team members continue to feel involved with, and responsible for, the overall objectives of the project. It is sometimes easier for those who have a preference for the 'bigger picture' rather than details to keep this in mind. However, there are risks associated with allowing

Figure 3.16 Project timeline

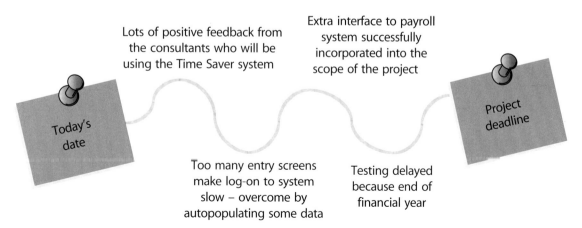

the team to concentrate only on their specialism and their deadlines. This ignores the interdependencies between the different pieces of work, and prevents team members from understanding how their contribution fits with other contributions to complete the deliverables of the project.

> **Real world experience**
>
> 'It's so easy for the team to fragment back to a group of individuals as people get really involved in their work. The team dynamic needs a purpose bigger than one particular piece of work to glue everyone together.'

A powerful way of getting team members engaged with the overall goals, deliverables and achievements of the project is to use a timeline game (Figure 3.16). During a team meeting, the team leader clears enough space in the room for all the team members to move about freely. The team leader puts a picture on the wall of the ultimate deliverable of the project, and the date by which it is to be delivered. If the date is very far in the future, the team leader might consider putting up other images of things that are happening in the world on that date, e.g. pictures of famous sporting fixtures that will take place, or notices about new laws that will have come into play by this time. In fact, anything that will help the team members picture themselves in the future. If a team member is due to have a baby or get married, pictures of this nature will also help.

The team leader stands at the front of the room and, along with all of the team members, goes and stands around the picture of the future. They talk about the successful delivery of the project, and all of the congratulations that the team are receiving, just as if the project had actually finished and the work was complete. Once everyone has mentally moved to this new date, they are asked to look at a sign on the other wall, which has today's date on it. They are then asked to look back and identify how they were successful: what work did they start with first, who did they work with and the hurdles that they had to overcome.

This is a simple and effective technique for ensuring that team members reconfirm in their own minds that the project will be successful, see themselves as part of that success and understand that the success is the achievement of the overall goal of the project and not just the piece of work that they are currently engaged with.

Team roles, responsibilities and processes

The team leader will need to clarify how the roles and responsibilities of each team member may change as the project moves on to the next stage. This can be a sensitive area of discussion. Although a quick look at the Project Plan indicates the change in emphasis of the project for the next stage, changing the responsibilities of a particular team member can be taken personally, as a reflection of the job that they have done in the last stage. When entering into these kinds of discussions, the team leader must keep this emotional agenda in mind, and ensure that their explanation does not cause any negative feelings.

As a programme moves into the next tranche, team members from projects that were completed in the previous tranche may be asked to form a new team for projects starting in this tranche. This means that an old team member will have to start again at the beginning of the team development stages, identifying the role that they will take in this new team. This role may have less 'power' or call on less of their specialist knowledge, which can trigger a grieving process whilst the team member adjusts to this new reality.

Case study: handling changing responsibilities

In the Time Saver project, the team member responsible for the design of the interfaces between the timekeeping system and the other business systems in operation in the consulting firm is now required to develop the processes to govern how the system will be used (Figure 3.17). The team leader needs to ensure this happens without any issues regarding the team member's capabilities.

Figure 3.17 Informing a team member about changing responsibilities without rancour

Team relationships

To continue to motivate the team members to stay focused on the project objectives whilst waiting on the decision from the sponsor and the decision-makers, the team leader can undertake some social and networking activities with them. This is a good opportunity to officially recognize the work completed to date, to say goodbye to the leaving members of the team, and to welcome the new members for the next stage (depending on the certainty of the decision-makers' determination to continue with the project). These interactions also help the team overcome any frustration felt about the periodic breaks in development for assessments.

Depending on the personalities involved, those joining and leaving the project can have a significant impact on the effectiveness of team relationships. These build up over time, and yet during the main stages of the project there is very little time to slowly get to know colleagues, as there is too much work to do in too little time. The team leader can reduce the disruption by planning the changes to the team, and how they will be addressed.

Case study: maintaining team relationships while waiting for authorization

The team leader of the Time Saver project is considering have a special event to thank those team members who are returning to their departments or supplier organizations, so that they leave in a spirit of goodwill. This will increase the chances that these team members are prepared to share what they have learnt, not only with the remaining members of the team, but also with any new joiners who will be at the event. So that the new joiners can meet the existing team members on neutral ground, the event is planned away from the office. The team leader knows this will increase the chance of social rather than purely work-related interaction, which will build relationships more quickly. It will also minimize the possible power base of the existing team members, which may appear daunting to those about to join the team. After all, no one really enjoys being the new child in class.

Figure 3.18 shows the information flows in an unmanaged situation.

Figure 3.18 Information flow – unmanaged

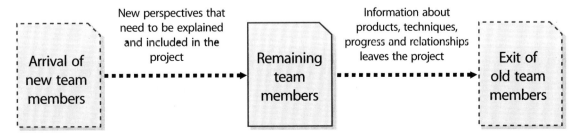

Figure 3.19 shows the information flows in a managed situation, where the atmosphere is kept positive and supportive.

3.9 CLOSING DOWN – EVALUATION

As a project comes to a close, there is a need to evaluate the usefulness of what the project delivered and the way in which it was delivered. The way in which the team operated together should be reviewed to see how the roles, responsibilities and relationships contributed to

project success, and how alignment of the team mission against the objectives of the project helped to ensure delivery of products that were fit for purpose. At the close of a programme, the programme manager will be working closely with the last remaining project teams. However, evaluation of the success of team working and team management must include all of the teams that were formed during the programme life.

Team mission and direction

During this last phase of the project, it is important for the team to remain focused on the objective of closing down the project properly. Once the final product has been completed and tested, there will be many outside pressures on the members to get back to their regular

Figure 3.19 Information flow – managed

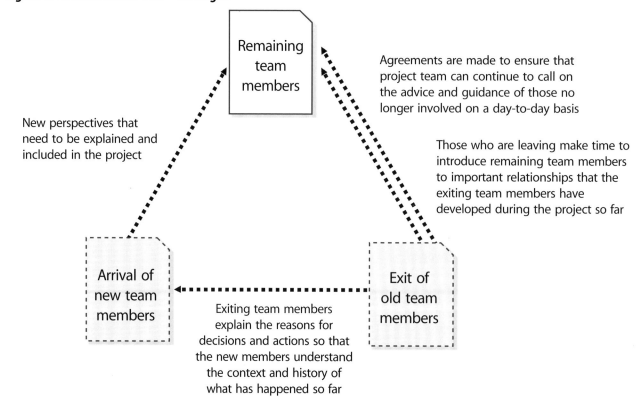

day jobs or move on to the next project. However, for the project and for the team, there needs to be some evaluation of performance and reflection on what the experience has given to the organization as a learning experience and to the individual team members in their own personal and professional development. Without this last step of closure, many important lessons learnt will be lost at a personal and organizational level.

The team leader needs to acknowledge that there are now two missions running simultaneously in the minds of the team members. One is the team mission but the other is the mission to find the next job or the next piece of work. Pretending that this personal objective does not exist is ignoring a valuable motivating factor that can be used to achieve the team goal.

Team roles, responsibilities and processes

One of the reasons that the team can start to dissolve early in the closure of the project, is that the roles and responsibilities are still centred on the creation of products and use of specialist skills. At the point of evaluation, team members should be given specific roles that relate to evaluation so that they take responsibility for this step and have a vested interest in carrying this out. To be as effective as possible, the team leader should consider how the team members are likely to disperse after the closure of the project, and ensure that their evaluation responsibilities will contribute to this.

Case study: ensuring lessons learned are passed on

One of the team members of the Time Saver project is going to join another project, with a similar set of outputs. They would gain value from evaluating the accuracy of the plans, the methods of estimating or the number of risks that were not terminated and became issues in this project. All of this information will be very useful when they come to plan the work of their next project. Another team member is returning to their operational role and they will find it helpful to take a lead in measuring the

benefits that the project has delivered, as the benefits result from the way in which the products delivered by the project are actually implemented and used within the operational environment.

Team relationships

The team will soon be disbanding and as team members begin to accept this, feelings of grieving are quite common, especially among members who have worked on the project from the start. The team leader can compensate for this feeling of ending by marking the successes of the project with an acknowledgement of work completed, a celebratory social activity, or by providing feedback to each individual who contributed. A final meeting to commemorate the project and the team assists those needing closure and provides the opportunity to give acknowledgement for successes.

3.10 CLOSING DOWN – HANDOVER

The key objective of this part of the project lifecycle is to ensure that operational staff who are responsible for using and operating the products created by the project have the support of the project team as knowledge about the products is transferred between the two groups. The objective of the team shifts from product creation to information sharing and coaching. Although this step will take place at the end of each tranche of a programme, the information is still applicable to each project within a programme.

Team mission and direction

At this point, the mission for the team moves from successful delivery to successful handover. The team leader must clearly state that the goals of the team have now changed, and ensure that the meaning of handover is fully understood by the team members, who may include members of the operational staff of the business. Just as there was a need to drill down and really explore the objectives of the project at start-up, the concept of handover must be developed to a similar level of detail. The specific goals and success criteria for handover must be established so that operational staff can start to identify how they can contribute.

Team roles, responsibilities and processes

The roles and responsibilities for the team members must be changed again, this time to allocate responsibilities for the handover. Successful closure of the project requires team members to move through several changes of role in a relatively short space of time, and the team leader may find resistance that is related to the quick change of roles, but also how far the roles are from what the team members are really concentrating on, which is their next job. As with the evaluation responsibilities, the team leader will need to generate interest in undertaking the handover responsibilities, and it is worth considering the question that may be running through the minds of the team members at this point: 'What's in it for me?'.

Case study: handing over effectively

The Time Saver team leader can show the connections between handover and the realization of the future that was promised at the start of the project. This may motivate those whose desire was to reach the destination and achieve the future. For those who are motivated by the journey, it is important to point out that there are still steps of the journey to enjoy, and new opportunities to work with operational staff and become involved in realizing the benefits that were promised by the project.

Team relationships

The team leader can rely on the relationships that have built up within the team to assist with handover, but if new team members join from the operational staff, the team leader will need to integrate them into existing team relationships. The buddy system could be used again, and time should be taken to listen to these staff so that their perspective can be understood and integrated in the approach to handover.

For example, these new members may have a great deal of understanding of the pressures on operational staff to keep the business running day to day, and can point out how handover impacts on their ability to complete their jobs. This background information on the atmosphere within the operational areas can be used to build relationships between the original project team members and those to whom they are handing over the use of the products.

In programme management, handover of project deliverables will happen multiple times, which means that the team leader must be very clear about when the responsibilities of the team members have moved from project delivery to project handover. There is also an increased need to ensure that the project teams and the operational staff form teams of their own to manage this handover, which means that the team leader must identify the specific goal for each of these teams, and select the most relevant members based on skills, experience and motivating factors.

Figure 3.20 shows how, in step 1, members of the project team and operational staff have a dialogue and work together, but remain separate teams. In step 2, members of the project team join the operational staff, and in step 3 this process is complete and there is one unified team that includes members from the original project team and the operational staff.

Figure 3.20 Team relationships in the handover stage

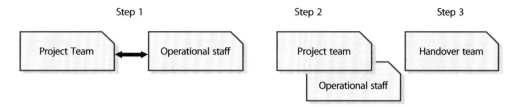

3.11 CLOSING DOWN – AUTHORIZATION

At this point in the project lifecycle, authorization is sought to close the project and officially disband the project team. There is nothing more for the team leader to do but to wish the team members well and then get ready to manage the next project team!

Appendices

Appendix A: Identifying different motivating factors

What motivates each of the team members is not an exact science. However, Table A.1 gives some clues, based on the names or phrases that a team member frequently uses to describe different situations.

Table A.1 Motivation can be driven by a range of factors

Using lessons learned	Stepping into the unknown
• In the past we have tried to do X	• We will be the first to comment on this
• We didn't have very good results with that approach	• We will be the first to see this
• There is a precedent for this	• There is no precedent for this
	• This is a chance to create a new approach
	• This is an opportunity to develop new ideas
	• This is a blank sheet of paper
Early adopters	**Those who need to be persuaded**
• I am going to do this right now	• What is the history to this?
• This sounds good, I will try it and let you know	• Who was involved in the decision?
• Lets just see what happens	• Did anyone else have input to this?
	• Is there any evidence that this will work?
	• Is there an example I can have a look at?
	• Have I got enough experience to carry this out?
	• Do I have the right skill set for this work?

Detailed instructions	Outline tasks
• The plan gives a detailed breakdown of the time, cost and resource estimates for each task	• The plan consists of three main activities
• If you have any issues, contact the operations director in the first instance, but include the finance director in any conference calls and copy her in on all emails	• If you have any issues, call the operations director
• The total cost will be £30,000, £10,000 of which are staff costs, and £5,000 has been set aside for possible changes	• It will cost £30,000

Operating in the present	Operating in the future
• I am doing ...	• I will do...
• This is my plan for today	• This is what I have achieved
• I am already busy finishing X	• The new processes are going to be very easy to use
• I cannot take on any other work until I have finished X	• I think everyone is going to like working on the new system

Motivated by the destination	Motivated by the journey
• I want to get this finished as soon as possible	• This task should give us a good opportunity to put the results of the workshop into practice
• Don't worry about finishing everything on the list, lets just make sure we have the basic structure ready as soon as possible	• I would like to give you a step-by-step breakdown of everything that this task will include
• If we hold the workshop next week, we should have everything finished by the end of the month.	• This is a good opportunity for me to use my risk analysis skills
• What is the estimated completion time?	• I am looking forward to working with the finance department because it will increase my understanding of the way they work
• How can we speed things up?	

Appendix B: Four practical tips for successful team management

This appendix contains tips and practical examples for the team management skills of:

- Meeting management
- Facilitation
- Time management
- Delegation.

Team members may also need to use these skills to contribute effectively to the team's progress and achievements and/or to lead sub-teams within the project.

B.1 MEETING MANAGEMENT

Meetings are a part of working in any team, so it is important that they are run effectively. One of the biggest complaints team members have about meetings is the wasted time and effort spent when they feel the project would have been better served by them working directly on the tasks. Meetings take time to prepare, time to attend and time to follow up. It is important to get the right mix of meetings versus other, possibly faster, communication methods.

Every meeting should have a clear purpose, which should be documented in an agenda that is circulated to all the participants prior to the meeting, with sufficient notification. An agenda helps set the participants' expectations about the topics being covered, the information they need to bring and possibly the decisions that will be made, and even whether they need to attend. Without this prior knowledge, participants may feel unprepared and consequently demotivated. This type of demoralization can cause team members to slip backwards in the team development stages, causing them to be less productive.

Some other essential factors for effective meetings that the team leader needs to be aware of are:

- Start on time and finish on time: the team leader (or whoever is chairing the meeting) needs to demonstrate respect for the team members by not wasting their time either waiting for the meeting to start or allowing it to overrun, and team members also need to show respect for their colleagues by arriving on time. If meetings always start on time, team members will get the message that they need to be there or risk missing important information or decisions that will have an impact on their work. If they always finish on time they will be more motivated to attend (as they can plan their other work around the meeting with confidence).
- Stay on track: the team leader (or whoever is chairing the meeting) needs to ensure that the purpose of the meeting remains the focus and they need to keep the discussion moving forward at an appropriate pace. A useful tip to avoid the purpose of the meeting being overtaken by other issues is to have a flipchart available, on which these other issues can be noted. The importance of these issues is recognized but as they are outside the scope of the meeting they can be addressed at a subsequent event. Whoever is taking the minutes of the meeting should capture these issues. This should help to ensure that there is sufficient time to deal with the agreed agenda items, allowing enough opportunity for team members to contribute to the discussion.
- Right people: meeting participants will feel frustrated if the people needed to discuss the agenda items are not at the meeting. It is important for the chair of the meeting to establish whether they will make

meeting attendance mandatory in order to avoid this happening. As mentioned earlier, having an agenda circulated prior to the meeting, clearly stating the purpose of the meeting, should help to alleviate this problem, as invitees should have ample time to raise the necessity of their attendance with the team leader if there is any doubt.

■ Progress: it is important that what has been achieved in the meeting is summarized and follow-up actions are agreed before the meeting ends. One way to ensure progress is to ask the minute taker to run through the agreed action points from the meeting, including who will do the actions and when they will be done by. This avoids any time lag between the end of the meeting and the minutes being circulated, and helps those with actions to progress them whilst the purpose is still fresh in their minds.

Meeting management does not end when the session ends. The team leader will need to ensure that the minutes are documented and circulated to all attendees and interested parties and that anything that needs to be documented is transferred to the appropriate documents, e.g. an uncovered risk needs to be added to the Risk Register and a new query to the Issues Log.

Finally, effective meeting management needs:

■ Someone to chair the meeting (whether the team leader or someone else). They must take charge of the meeting, guide the attendees to keep them on track, and ensure that the key points are noted and circulated.

■ Someone to take notes on key decisions and agreed next steps. Unless you have the luxury of a project administration resource, it is a good idea to vary who takes on this role at each meeting as it can restrict participation in a meeting and cause frustration.

■ Someone to keep an eye on time (this could be the team leader or the minute taker) to make sure that all the agenda items can be covered before the

allotted meeting time is up. This is easier to achieve if the agenda items have suggested amounts of time allocated to them.

B.2 FACILITATION SKILLS

During projects or programmes, a team leader or team member may be asked to facilitate a workshop or a part of a meeting. The audiences for these can range from team members, stakeholders, sub-teams and related project teams to users or third-party suppliers. Sometimes a facilitated discussion can be the entire focus of the gathering, such as a project definition workshop with the entire project team, or it could be based on one agenda item in a team meeting, where the team leader will need to change from chairing the meeting to facilitating the discussion. The distinction between the two is slight, but imperative. In order to facilitate, that is to guide a discussion without personally taking one side or the other, the designated facilitator must remain objective while helping the group obtain its objectives.

Qualities of a good facilitator

A good facilitator needs to remain neutral throughout the meeting. If the facilitator has an inherent interest in a certain outcome, then an outside facilitator may be required. A facilitator differs from a team leader but both need to have good meeting management skills, and in team meetings the team leader often assumes the facilitator role. A facilitator will demonstrate leadership skills by focusing the group on the agenda topics, stimulating and encouraging discussions and participation. They must also demonstrate mediation skills by maintaining order throughout the meeting or workshop, discouraging participants from dominating the discussion and ensuring that everyone is given an opportunity to contribute, all while maintaining a neutral stance on the topic under discussion.

A good facilitator pays particular attention to the behaviours of the individuals involved, and relies on the use of questions to probe or stimulate discussion, especially from the more introverted or quiet members. He or she is able to discern what needs to be done to allow everyone to have their say, whilst keeping an eye on the clock and the achievement of the task in hand. This way of operating requires the facilitator to be self-confident, and have confidence in the participants and in the process.

B.3 TIME MANAGEMENT SKILLS

Time management entails a three-pronged approach to managing the team's activities efficiently over time (Figure B.1). It involves knowing how to plan, being diligent about working against the plan and making adjustments when necessary. Managing time is everyone's responsibility. The team leader will help the members stay focused on the team's plan, but each individual will need to ensure that their tasks are completed in accordance to that plan.

Figure B.1 The three-pronged approach to time management

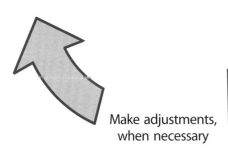

Know how to plan

Be diligent about working against the plan

Make adjustments, when necessary

Knowing how to plan

A major principle behind Project Plans is that they continue to be broken down into shorter, more detailed, more manageable plans until the activities are small enough to be estimated accurately. Because the process starts with planning a high-level overview of the entire work, which then gets broken down into smaller and smaller segments, these segments are guaranteed to be subsets of the overall work and thus contribute to its objectives.

Knowing how to plan means that the team members must understand the objectives of the work involved. Using their specialist or expert knowledge they must break it down into manageable pieces and map these activities onto a timeline based on the agreed priorities. When putting together a plan, it is essential to involve the people who will be producing the work. They are often the ones most able to accurately forecast task duration based on previous experience, and there is an additional benefit in that it builds commitment to the plan and ownership of the task.

Working to the plan

To be diligent about working to the plan involves having a mechanism to monitor progress against the agreed plan, and time should be allocated for this activity as well as for completing the project tasks themselves. Providing accurate and timely progress information requires commitment from all involved to be organized in their approach to the work. Honesty in providing progress data is essential. If problems are not being reported or are being intentionally hidden, then the team will have lost control over its time management.

If producers of work are feeling tight on time, stopping the flow of work to report progress seems counterproductive, and therefore the reporting of the work tends to slip. If the reporting arrangements have been planned for, it is more likely that the reports will be received at the agreed intervals.

Making timely adjustments

When the actual work falls behind the plan, adjustments will be needed. The team will need to understand the severity and impact of the slippages before taking any corrective action. This represents the link between time management and issue management. When an issue arises, it is important to understand its impact before deciding whether or when to spend time correcting it. When it is deemed necessary to fix within the team's given constraints, then this indicates one or more of the priorities of the work will have changed. The team leader will need to ensure that this switch in priorities is communicated to those affected by it.

If the situation caused by the deviation from the plan cannot be remedied by the team within their given constraints, it must be escalated to the next higher authority in the organization structure to take a decision about correcting it.

The best way to manage the use of time is to apply a plan–do–review method. Plan the work ahead, execute the plan and periodically review progress, making adjustments as needed. This method can be used at the individual, team and organizational levels.

Methods of prioritizing work

A common strategy for planning work involves prioritizing the work activities and allocating time to complete them, based on their importance/urgency ratio (Covey, 1989; Figure B.2).

Anything that is 'Urgent and important' should be addressed immediately and completed as quickly as possible. These are often the fire-fighting activities that arise during a project that need immediate attention, such as a misunderstanding of a specification between a project team member and an external solution supplier. If these types of situation arise frequently, this should alert the team leader that there is a procedural problem within the project or programme that will need to be addressed. The team leader whose attention is constantly diverted to deal with urgent and important matters will have less capacity for the significant tasks of the project or programme, such as stakeholder or supplier management, which could be a risk to the overall achievement of the objectives.

Figure B.2 The importance/urgency ratio for prioritizing activities within a project

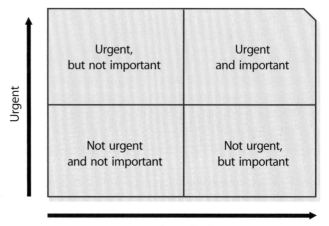

'Urgent but not important' activities should be delegated to someone else. These tasks must be completed, but because their importance is low, the responsibility of doing them can be delegated to someone else, and there may also be a potential benefit of delegating them to someone with previous experience of this activity. By sharing these tasks with the team, the team leader's time can be freed up to address the remaining important tasks. However, it is important to delegate the task properly, explaining the reason why it is being given to the relevant person, to ensure that they do not feel that they are being dumped on!

'Not urgent but important' activities will usually require the most time to handle. The procedural problem mentioned earlier may fall under this category. Sufficient time and energy will be required to research and resolve these items. These actions usually involve bigger picture thinking because they tend to affect more than one area or department. Involvement of others in these tasks is usually the best approach.

Finally, items under 'Not urgent and not important' should be discarded or eliminated as they are usually time-wasting efforts with little or no value.

B.4 DELEGATION SKILLS

Once the work has been divided into manageable pieces, it can be delegated to the appropriate resources to take on the responsibility of completing it. Delegation involves assigning a group or an individual a piece of work and, by doing so, passing on the responsibility, but not the accountability, for completing the work (Figure B.3).

Figure B.3 Delegating responsibility

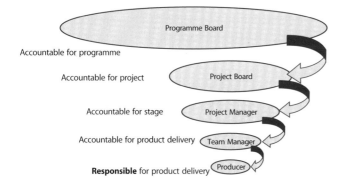

Accountable for programme

Accountable for project

Accountable for stage

Accountable for product delivery

Responsible for product delivery

Programme Board

Project Board

Project Manager

Team Manager

Producer

There is a delicate balance to achieve when delegating work. Too much involvement or too many detailed instructions from the delegator leads to micromanagement which is constraining, stifling and ineffective. However, too little involvement or too few instructions can result in confusion and increase the likelihood that the work is either not completed or completed incorrectly.

Delegation, if done well, promotes the development of capacity in team members which will ultimately benefit, if not this project, then the next one the person is involved in. Team leaders should consider whether they can delegate a task in such a way that the person taking it on still has choice, for example in the way that the task is done, as long as they still produce the desired outcome.

Accountability versus responsibility

Accountability entails being answerable for or liable to another person or party, whereas responsibility entails the act of doing or performing a function satisfactorily. Often, project and programme managers do not undertake the specialist work associated with project and programme delivery. Instead they delegate the responsibility of doing the work to the levels of management below them.

Another distinction between accountability and responsibility lies in the ability to take decisions about the piece of work involved. Responsible parties perform or produce the work, whilst accountable parties are able to change the nature of the work or take decisions about the work. Striking the right balance in delegation means the team leader who is delegating work must provide clear instructions, be clear about the constraints for the work and be realistic about their expectations. Similarly, those being delegated to should receive clear instructions and details of the constraints around the work, and they should be realistic about what they can and cannot accomplish within those constraints. An agreement between the two parties is essential as it ensures that both parties have understood who is going to do what.

Though verbal instructions are sometimes acceptable as a method of delegation, it is usually best practice to back these up with something in writing, such as an email. When working with third-party suppliers, many organizations require a full procurement process which includes signing off a detailed contract. However, when delegating work to internal resources, it is easy to become lax with instructions, which creates a potential threat to a successful outcome.

The use of a written work request ensures that the delegate receives all the necessary information to complete the work, such as the product descriptions, constraints, quality standards, progress reporting arrangements, configuration management requirements and problem handling procedures. By having this information before the work is required, the delegate can determine if it is possible and realistic. Some amount of influencing and/or negotiation may be required in order to come to an agreement about the work being requested.

Successful delegation

The following activities help promote successful delegation, which is measured by the satisfactory achievement of the task objective.

Choose the right person

When delegating a piece of work to someone, the team leader must ensure that the person has the skills to do the work or be given appropriate training to develop these skills. The person selected must have sufficient availability to do the work as well as their existing commitments. If the new task has a higher priority, investigate the possibility of re-assigning some of their existing work. The team leader should be prepared to make an effort to gain the team member's buy-in to the priority of the task.

Clearly define and communicate the task

Written documentation that explains the work involved is the best way to reduce miscommunications. However, time and effort still needs to be allocated to discussing, clarifying and possibly negotiating the conditions or constraints surrounding the work. It may be appropriate to get an official agreement before the delegate starts the work, whether informal and oral, or formal and written.

Be available

It is an implied condition of delegation that the delegator must make reasonable time provision to provide feedback on work done and be available for problems or issues the team member may encounter. This is important for the motivation of the person doing the task. This does not imply the delegator has to be involved in completing the work, but means they have to be aware of the progress.

Progress reports or meetings to ensure progress is being made help the delegator to understand the time and effort that is being given to the work. If the progress is satisfactory, the team leader should take the opportunity to praise the person. However, if the progress is not acceptable, the delegator needs to make themselves available as soon as possible. Immediate attention is required to help resolve problems or issues.

Allow for creativity

In order for the delegate to take ownership for the work involved, there needs to be flexibility to allow for creativity in how the work is approached. Just because the delegate does not approach the work in the same manner that the delegator would do it, does not mean that it is wrong. It is simply different. And as long as the progress information continues to indicate that the work will be completed within the agreed constraints (time, cost and quality), then the delegator should stand back from over-managing or micro-managing the process.

Reward good performance

When a delegate has successfully completed the agreed work, they should be recognized for it. This builds confidence and enthusiasm within the delegate to do similar work in the future. For extraordinary work that goes above and beyond expectations, the team leader should ensure that the team member's line manager is made aware of their contributions and achievements.

Appendix C: Stages of team development

Based on the work of Tuckman (1965) it has been established that when groups of people form teams, they go through a number of team development stages. Teams start with a bit of angst about why the team exists, what role they are going to play and who the other members are. After the initial excitement, members will endure a bit of a frustrating period where they feel uncertain about what they should be doing and how they are going to get on with the other team members. Once the relationships are fully established, they begin to fuse together as a team, fully understanding their role and their contributions. The team then reaches a fulfilment stage in its development, where the team members can trust each other and share openly and work collaboratively towards their objectives. When a project or programme draws to a close, the teams involved will move into the final stage of development, where they disband and possibly experience a sense of loss.

The leader needs to manage and facilitate the team through these development stages, which are characterized in this publication by the five Fs:

- Familiarization (Figure C.1)
- Frustration (Figure C.2)
- Fusion (Figure C.3)
- Fulfilment (Figure C.4)
- Finishing.

Familiarization

Team members feel uneasy and nervous about the team, its goals, the leader, and the other members. For many on the team, the idea of starting something new is exciting, so motivation is high.

Regardless of how eager they are to start, each team member will require one-to-one meetings with their leader to voice their opinions in a safe environment before they are willing to share them with the rest of the team.

Figure C.1 Familiarization – getting to know each other

Frustration

Team members grow disenchanted with the team, their role and/or the leader. Team members may develop a sense that the objectives are too far-reaching, leading to panic, anxiety or discontent. The team members are still feeling unsure of each other and are still trying to understand who the true leader is, be it the formal team leader or another team member. This phase may involve posturing and some office politics until the individual members are able to establish their own role, identity, importance and contribution to the team.

Figure C.2 Frustration – people jostle for position within the team and try to establish relationships

Fusion

After a period of displeasure, the team members iron out their differences and establish their roles, and start to come together for the greater good of the team and begin focusing on their objectives.

Figure C.3 Fusion – roles are established and relationships form

Fulfilment

When the team members have come together and are working as a unit towards their objectives, they have reached the fulfilment phase of team development. The team members may conduct actual work in isolation or in conjunction with sub-teams, but they rely on each other for support and help with the completion of the team's work. Throughout the process of team development, the goal has been to reach this stage; however, care and attention continue to be required to manage the team. Without the appropriate advice and reinforcement from the leader, the team may fall backwards in the team development stages.

When new team members join, the existing relationships can break, and the team may return to the stages of Familiarization or Frustration before new relationships are formed and the team can complete the Fusion stage and move forward into Fulfilment.

Figure C.4 Fulfilment – team members may work together or in isolation, but they rely on each other for support and help in completing the work

Finishing

A fifth stage of team development occurs when the team disbands due to the project completing, or the decision taken by the sponsor and decision-makers to prematurely close the project or programme down. This stage might also be invoked when key members of the team leave. Team members may experience grief and mourning at the closing of the team environment that has been created. They might go through anxiety over leaving their new friends and colleagues and about starting new projects or going back to their regular jobs. It is important to provide an opportunity for members to acknowledge the ending and have some closure.

References

- Covey, S.R. (1989). *The Seven Habits of Highly Effective People: Powerful Lessons in Personal Change.* New York, New York: Fireside.
- Katzenbach, J.R., Smith, D.K. (1993). *The discipline of teams. Harvard Business Review May–June*, 95–103.
- Tuckman, B.W. (1965). *Development sequence in small groups. Psychological Bulletin* 63: 284–299.

Glossary

Glossary

Activity
An activity is a process, function or task that occurs over time, has recognizable results and is managed.

Benefit
The measurable improvement resulting from an outcome perceived as an advantage by one or more stakeholders.

Business as usual
The way the business normally achieves its objectives.

Business change manager
The role responsible for benefits management, from identification through to realization, ensuring the implementation and embedding of the new capabilities delivered by the projects. Typically allocated to more than one individual. Alternative title: 'change agent'.

Customer
The person or group who commissioned the work and will benefit from the end results.

Deliverable
An item that the project has to create as part of the requirements. It may be part of the final outcome or an intermediate element on which one or more subsequent deliverables are dependent. According to the type of project, another name for a deliverable is 'product'.

Impact
Impact is the result of a particular threat or opportunity actually occurring.

Issue
A relevant event that has happened, was not planned, and requires management action. Could be a problem, query, concern, change request or risk that has occurred.

Issue log
Contains all project issues including Requests for Change raised during the project. Project issues are each allocated a unique number and are filed in the issue log under the appropriate status.

Opportunity
An uncertain event that could have a favourable impact on objectives or benefits.

Outcome
The result of change, normally affecting real-world behaviour and/or circumstances. Outcomes are desired when a change is conceived. Outcomes are achieved as a result of the activities undertaken to effect the change. In a programme, the outcome is the manifestation of part or all of the new state conceived in the blueprint.

Output
The tangible or intangible product resulting from a planned activity.

Phase
A part, section or segment of a project, similar in meaning to a PRINCE2 stage. The key meaning of stage in PRINCE2 terms is the use of management stages, i.e. sections of the project to which the Project Board only commits one at a time. A phase might be more connected to a time slice, change of skills required or change of emphasis.

Phase
A part, section or segment of a project, similar in meaning to a PRINCE2 stage. The key meaning of stage in PRINCE2 terms is the use of management stages, i.e. sections of the project to which the Project Board only commits one at a time. A phase might be more connected to a time slice, change of skills required or change of emphasis.

Plan
A detailed proposal for doing or achieving something detailing the what, when, how and by whom.

Product
An input or output, whether tangible or intangible, that can be described in advance, created and tested. Also known as an output or deliverable.

Programme

A temporary flexible organization structure created to coordinate, direct and oversee the implementation of a set of related projects and activities in order to deliver outcomes and benefits related to the organization's strategic objectives. A programme is likely to have a life that spans several years.

Project

A temporary organization that is created for the purpose of delivering one or more business products according to a specified Business Case.

Project lifecycle

The period from the start up of a project to the handover of the finished product to those who will operate and maintain it.

Project manager

The person given the authority and responsibility to manage the project on a day-to-day basis to deliver the required products within the constraints agreed with the Project Board.

Project Plan

A high-level plan showing the major products of the project, when they will be delivered and at what cost. An initial project plan is presented as part of the Project Initiation Document. This is revised as information on actual progress appears. It is a major control document for the Project Board to measure actual progress against expectations.

Project support

An administrative role in the project management team. Project support can be in the form of advice and help with project management tools, guidance, administrative services such as filing, and the collection of actual data. The provision of any project support on a formal basis is optional. Tasks either need to be done by the project manager or delegated to a separate body and this will be driven by the needs of the individual project and project manager.

Risk

An uncertain event or set of events which, should it occur, will have an effect on the achievement of objectives. A risk is measured by a combination of the probability of a perceived threat or opportunity occurring and the magnitude of its impact on objectives.

Risk Log

See Risk Register.

Risk Register

A record of identified risks relating to an initiative, including their status and history.

Senior responsible owner

The single individual with overall responsibility for ensuring that a project or programme meets its objectives and delivers the projected benefits.

Senior supplier

The Project Board role that provides knowledge and experience of the main discipline(s) involved in the production of the project's deliverable(s). Represents the supplier interests within the project and provides supplier resources.

Senior user

The Project Board role accountable for ensuring that user needs are specified correctly and that the solution meets those needs.

Sponsor

The main driving force behind a programme or project.

Sponsoring group

The main driving force behind a programme who provide the investment decision and top-level endorsement of the rationale and objectives of the programme.

Stage

A stage is the section of the project that the project manager is managing on behalf of the Project Board at any one time, at the end of which the Project Board may review progress to date, the state of the Project Plan, Business Case and risks, and the next stage plan in order to decide whether to continue with the project.

Stakeholder

Any individual, group or organization that can affect, be affected by, or perceive itself to be affected by, an initiative (programme, project, activity, risk).

Strategy

The approach or line to take, designed to achieve a long-term aim. Strategies can exist at different levels in an organization – in *Managing Successful Programmes* there are corporate strategies for achieving objectives that will give rise to programmes. Programmes then develop strategies aligned with these corporate objectives against particular delivery areas.

Supplier

The group or groups responsible for the supply of the project's specialist products.

Team manager

A role that may be adopted by the project manager or senior supplier to manage the work of project team members.

Tranche

A group of projects structured around distinct step changes in capability and benefit delivery.

Index

Index